# PHILOSOPHY
## *Wise*

### TIMELESS IDEAS FOR A MEANINGFUL LIFE

D1600942

First paperback edition October 2021

BOOK DESIGN BY
Letícia Naves

ILLUSTRATIONS BY
Helena Cintra

PRINTED BY

ISBN 978-1-7374257-0-0 (paperback)

ISBN 978-1-7374257-1-7 (eBook)

ISBN 978-1-7374257-2-4 (audio)

philosophywise.com

# PHILOSOPHY
## *Wise*

TIMELESS IDEAS
FOR A
MEANINGFUL
LIFE

## *Sharin N. Elkholy, PhD*

INSIGHT, WISDOM, AND GUIDANCE
FROM **20** OF THE WORLD'S
GREATEST MINDS

*For Leilah*
*Whose Wisdom Truly Surpasses Her Years*
*And For Which I Am Grateful*

# CONTENTS

# ALSO BY SHARIN N. ELKHOLY, PhD

*The Philosopher's Deck and Guidebook*

*Heidegger and a Metaphysics of Feeling: Angst and the Finitude of Being*

*The Philosophy of the Beats, ed.*

COMPLETE LIST OF PUBLICATIONS

https://uhd.academia.edu/SharinElkholy

# ACKNOWLEDGMENTS

Distilling the philosophical ideas that have guided and given meaning to my life into what is now *Philosophy Wise* has been an ongoing project of mine. I would like to thank my professors at Antioch College and The New School for Social Research, especially Dr. Pat Linn and Dr. James Dodd, for putting me on the path of questioning and allowing me to grow as a thinker. I thank my students at the University of Houston—Downtown for helping me demonstrate the practical relevance of the ideas discussed here. My daughter Leilah, I thank for her patience and work in helping me to clarify my thoughts. I thank Gillian Murphy, Sam Antoci, and Mike Diamond for their feedback and proofreading. Most of all, I thank my former student Joe Singleton for his editing help, with providing endnotes, and invaluable support in helping to bring this project to completion. I would also like to dedicate this work to Magda.

# PHILOSOPHY WISE
## INTRODUCTION

People used to think that philosophy could tell them how to live a more meaningful life. Not many people believe that today. Our conversations are less and less concerned with philosophy and its pursuit of wisdom, self-examination, and ethical practices, and more and more focused on the values of material and financial reward. Modern culture seems to have forgotten what philosophy can do, and the gifts it offers the soul. Perhaps philosophy has forgotten its own wisdom. Obscured by over-specializations and professional jargon, philosophy's messages remain mysterious, shrouded by complex language, and hidden within university walls. This is concerning because with the loss of philosophical insights, we lose valuable guides that have helped us navigate life for thousands of years. Philosophy should not be reduced to a laborious academic exercise available to only a few. Philosophy belongs to all of us. It is a tool with the power to radically inform and transform our lives.

At heart, to philosophize is to practice the art of living well. In Ancient Greek, philosophy simply means the love (*philos*) of wisdom (*sophia*). Of course, philosophers don't have a monopoly on life's big questions. But the ideas that arise from contemplating the good life are the materials with which philosophers work. And ideas matter. They shape how we think and how we see ourselves, others, and the world. We might say that philosophy is to the mind what physical exercise is to the body.

*Philosophy Wise* brings the wonder of philosophical ideas into your everyday life. Re-invigorating philosophy's initial purpose to provide guidance for better living, this book invites you to join in conversation with seekers of wisdom who will help you flourish and build your own philosophy of life. Written for philosophers and non-philosophers alike, *Philosophy Wise* demonstrates how your concerns and questions can be approached philosophically to allow you to think more clearly and consciously about nearly everything. Philosophy doesn't just provide answers, it teaches you how to think for yourself. At times, simply understanding your circumstances without even changing them can significantly improve your life. Some ideas in this book will be inspiring, some will elicit a deeper level of realization, and some will incite you to action. All the ideas presented here will expose you to more enduring ways of thinking, living, and seeing the world.

*Philosophy Wise* introduces 20 philosophers whose ideas have stood the test of time to serve as models of wisdom and practical conduct. Each thinker will offer different formulas for good living presented here in an accessible style. At the end of each chapter you will find a section illustrating how to apply the ideas to your life, followed by a series of thought-provoking questions. Pick and choose from among the kaleidoscope of ideas to provoke clarity, guidance, and inspiration. *Philosophy Wise's* unique approach emphasizes the reader as it repurposes complex ideas into tools for daily living. The only thinker that this book asks you to go deep with is you. If you want to engage with these ideas more playfully, you can turn to the *Philosopher's Deck.* There you will find a beautifully illustrated set of cards depicting each philosopher, including an extra two thinkers and an accompanying *Guidebook.* The *Deck* may be used to spark intuition and meditation through art and visualization; the *Guidebook* to further advise on how to incorporate philosophical viewpoints into your journey.

Embrace who you are and become the artist of your own life. Use these philosopher guides to clarify your reflections on what matters most to you. Engaging with the thoughts in this book will strengthen the muscles of your mind and empower you to live a richer and more fulfilling life. These philosophers were indeed mavericks; many of them risked their lives and reputations to develop new possibilities for how to live. Lend them your ear and experiment with their radical ideas. From Socrates to Camus, from Eastern to Western thought, the insights in *Philosophy Wise* can endow your life with meaning—and meaning makes a remarkable difference to the thinking and talking beings that we are.

# Socrates

470 BCE GREECE    399 BCE GREECE

## *The Unexamined Life Is Not Worth Living*

Socrates is a ~~philosopher of self-examination~~. He asks us to engage in regular dialogue with ourselves and others to examine the values that guide our lives. Two of his most fundamental beliefs—that "the unexamined life is not worth living," and that a good life is a virtuous life—have come to define what it means to live a philosophical life. They present us with a bold challenge to live our lives with conviction by putting the truths and values we take for granted to the test. By identifying our beliefs and knowing why we believe what we do, we come to understand what we deem important and what makes our lives worth living. Self-examination allows us to live more purposeful lives. Without it we would not know who we are, or the meaning and value of our lives.

So that he could devote his time to learning and teaching, Socrates embraced poverty. Unlike most of his fellow Athenians, he was not concerned with accumulating wealth or power but with the pursuit of wisdom and what it means to live a good life: "the most important thing is not life, but the good life."[1] To all appearances Socrates looked like a fool. Barefoot, unkempt, snub-nosed, and rather unattractive, he could easily have been mistaken for a hobo or a madman. Indeed, the philosopher Friedrich Nietzsche portrayed him as just that: "Socrates was the buffoon who got himself taken seriously[.]"[2] Yet Socrates drew the ire of the wealthiest and most powerful men in Athens. They felt threatened by his unconventional practice of self-examination and his willingness to sacrifice material pleasures for his ideals. They also feared the impact his teachings would have on the youth of Athens. His incessant questioning and call to care for the soul challenged Athenian traditions and, most fundamentally, the authority of those in power. "O my friend, why do you who are a citizen of the great and mighty and wise city of Athens, care so much about laying up the greatest amount of money and honor and reputation, and so little about wisdom and truth and the greatest improvement of the soul, which you never regard or heed at all? Are you not ashamed of this?"[3]

Socrates placed himself under constant self-examination and forced others around him to do the same. Without self-examination there can be no integrity: self-awareness through self-examination is the way to a satisfied life. Socrates likens himself to a midwife, helping us to give birth to wisdom and self-knowledge. He asks us to think for ourselves and live virtuously: "For I go around doing nothing but persuading both young and old among you not to care for your body or your wealth . . . but for the best possible state of your soul[.]"[4] Along this journey, he collected a fair number of enemies.

Attracted by Socrates's charisma and his project of self-examination, the children of the elite gathered to hear him speak. This may be partly why wealthy Athenians accused him of corrupting the youth and claiming to know everything. But for Socrates, questioning was a way of life. He took nothing for granted, and assumed that all previous knowledge was tainted by politics, economics, or custom. In his quest for knowledge, he found that those who were reputed to be wise often appeared so to themselves and others but did not in fact know what they claimed to know. "So I left him, saying to myself, as I went away: well, although I do not suppose that either of us knows anything really beautiful and good, I am better off than he is for he knows nothing, and thinks that he knows. I neither know nor think that I know."[5]

Socrates's practice of questioning has come to be called the Socratic method—a method meant to stimulate critical thinking by volleying ideas back and forth to make sure they are consistent and able to stand the test of reason. Through this method, Socrates was able to expose his disputers' inconsistencies and the lack of rational support for their positions. Confounded by his questioning, the supposedly wise Athenians were often left scrambling to protect their reputations. This led to Socrates being branded a dangerous mind. Yet his aim was not to win arguments, but to show how little human wisdom matters in the grand scheme of things. This is likely why the great Oracle at Delphi named him the wisest man in Athens. "What is probable, gentlemen, is that in fact the god is wise and that his oracular response meant that human wisdom is worth little or nothing, and that when he says this man, Socrates, he is using my name as an example, as if he said: 'This man among you, mortals, is wisest who, like Socrates, understand that his wisdom is worthless.'"[6]

Conscious of the limitations of his knowledge, Socrates remains eternally curious and open to learning from others. Recognizing that his wisdom lay in the awareness of his own lack of knowledge, he embarks upon a never ending path toward new possibilities and ways of understanding. When we concede that we do not know everything, we open ourselves up to the unknown and to growing. Indeed, our knowledge is little compared to the enormity of all there is to know. While others claim to know what they do not, Socrates wisely claims to know nothing: "I am likely to be wiser than he to this small extent, that I do not think I know what I do not know."[7] Socrates teaches us that a good life is defined by how we live and not by what we know or have. His concern was not with accumulating knowledge, but with changing the way people think and live.

Socrates compares himself to a gadfly, sent by the gods to awaken the Athenians from their deep sleep and to teach them that happiness comes only from the awareness of doing the right thing: "I never cease to rouse each and every one of you, to persuade and reproach you all day long[.] ... You might easily be annoyed with me as people are when they are aroused from a doze, and strike out at me; if convinced by Anytus you could easily kill me, and then you could sleep on for the rest of your days, unless the god, in his care for you, sent you someone else."[8] We can either choose to sleepwalk through life, caring about material gain and what others tell us to care about, or, like Socrates, we may examine for ourselves what it means to live a good life of virtue.

Socrates was illiterate and wrote down nothing. Thanks to his student Plato, who cast Socrates as the protagonist in his philosophical dialogues, we have an account of Socrates's dialectical style of searching for the truth. In Plato's "Allegory of the Cave," Socrates describes the difficulty of waking people up to the truth. He depicts a group of prisoners in an underground cave, there since childhood, with their legs and necks in chains. Unable to turn their heads, they see only the shadows of images projected on a wall by puppeteers who stand unseen behind them. They take these shadows and projected images to be reality: "To them the truth would be literally nothing but the shadows of the images." The prisoners busy themselves by naming these shadows and identifying patterns—even having competitions over who can identify them first. Never asking questions about their environment, world, or how they got to where they are, they simply accept the lives that are given to them.

One day, Socrates explains, a prisoner is set free. Fearing to leave what is familiar, he needs a push to exit the cave. As he makes his way from the cave, he struggles to adjust his sight to the light outside. At first, he turns his gaze downward, looking at the shadows familiar to him from his time in the cave. He then lifts his eyes to see the reflection of objects in the water before looking eventually at the things themselves. Finally, he turns his sight upward toward the sun and comes to the realization that it is the source that illuminates all he sees. Here Plato uses the symbol of the sun to represent the light of reason and its ability to go beyond knowledge acquired by the senses to the contemplation of absolute and universal truths.

The "Allegory of the Cave" aims to direct our sights upward toward the care of our souls. For Socrates, what really matters cannot be materially seen or measured by the pleasures attained through our senses. What matters is living a virtuous and principled life. This kind of awakening is radical and requires a complete rotation in the soul: a rotation equivalent to the prisoner's difficult journey out of the darkness of the cave. Some of us will stay in the cave our whole lives, believing only what we are given without questioning what we see or hear. Like the prisoners, we remain in the dark while allowing those with authority to fill our heads with ideas. Indeed, awakening to a principled life may put us at odds with the more material values promoted by society. This is why self-examination requires courage and a commitment to stand independently from the crowd and act upon what we know is right. Were the freed prisoner to return to liberate the others from the darkness of the cave, Socrates imagines, he would be met by hostility. "And, as for anyone who tried to free them and lead them upward, if they could somehow get their hands on him, wouldn't they kill him?"[9] Indeed, this is ultimately what happened to Socrates.

To silence him, Socrates was brought to trial on the spurious charges of corrupting the youth and believing in false gods. His quest for truth in the face of established facts and long held beliefs angered those in power, who eventually sentenced him to death. Although he was offered the opportunity to plea for his life and go into exile, Socrates refused. He stayed faithful to his beliefs and principles. Socrates told the jury that he would likely meet the same fate in an exiled land, for he would never cease his mission of reproaching others to care for their souls. Claiming never to know what he didn't know, Socrates did not fear death, the great unknown. What he did fear is what he knew to be wrong: an unexamined and unvirtuous life. "The difficulty, my friends, is not in avoiding death, but in avoiding unrighteousness; for that runs faster than death."[10] Indeed, Socrates even welcomed death, declaring that if an afterlife existed he would have the opportunity to examine the great minds of the past. "Nay, if this be true, let me die again and again . . . I shall be able to continue my search into true and false knowledge; as in this world, so also in that; I shall find out who is wise, and who pretends to be wise, and is not . . . What infinite delight would there be in conversing with them and asking them questions!"[11]

Socrates asks us to search for the roots of our happiness in virtuous living. Caring little for material comforts, what mattered to him was wisdom and virtue. Ironically, he met Nietzsche's greatest measure for affirming life: wishing for nothing in his life to be different. By demonstrating that he would do in the afterlife exactly what he had done while living—questioning people regarding the state of their souls—he testified to the value of his life. Having consciously chosen to live what he deemed a good life, Socrates mastered the art of dying free of regret. At the late age of 70, surrounded by friends in his jail cell, he drank a cup of hemlock, sealing his fate forever as a martyr for philosophy—the love (*philos*) of wisdom (*sophia*).

know that you do
not know

open yourself to expand
what you do know

# APPLYING SOCRATES' PHILOSOPHY

Socrates wants you to live a life of conviction. He rouses you out of your everyday routines by pushing you to look at your life using the tool of self-examination. Self-examination is the path toward self-knowledge. It requires a conversation with yourself—a dialogue between different ideas and perspectives. Don't ignore the moments that cause you to pause and examine your life. Awaken to the values that define your life and live as virtuously and as self-consciously as possible. Scrutinizing and reflecting on your beliefs allows you to live in the light of your convictions without apology. Direct your attention away from the values of wealth, power and fame, and toward the care of your soul. Knowing who you are and what you stand for is how you live a more satisfying life. Through self-reflection guided by a commitment to live a good life through virtuous activity, you are able to give your life meaning and purpose. For Socrates, virtue and happiness are one.

Ponder the riddle that Socrates gives you: he is the wisest because he realizes that he knows nothing, and knows too that human wisdom is worth little in the great scheme of things. On the surface, this statement appears ironic. Yet Socrates shows that the most important things lie beyond what you think you know. Don't close your mind and confine your thinking to fixed answers or conclusions. Open yourself to new ideas and broaden your perspective by questioning and engaging in conversation with yourself and others. Wisdom lies in knowing what you don't know. Aware of your own ignorance, you are ready to learn from others and from experience. Socrates wants you to be able to die peacefully, knowing that you have lived your life with care and consideration, and are therefore free from regret. Think about whether, like Socrates, you can claim confidently that you would do exactly what you are doing now in the afterlife, if one were to exist. Living your life with a view toward death will guide you toward living with purpose now.

# QUESTIONS FOR CONSIDERATION

- *Do you take time to examine how you live your life?*

- *Have you chosen your life with purpose?*

- *Do you ask yourself what it means to live a good life?*

- *Is your time spent seeking material goods, or pursuing the Socratic good life: the life of wisdom and virtue through life-long questioning and self-examination?*

- *Are you following common blueprints for life and adopting values that have been handed down to you over time without question or examination?*

- *What are the values that guide and give meaning to your life?*

- *Do you have confidence in the path that you have chosen, a confidence born out of examination and self-inspection?*

- *Do you stop yourself from learning because you think you already know everything?*

- *How would you live your life differently if you adopted the Socratic stance of ignorance?*

- *What are some of the lessons you have learned from your own mistakes?*

- *Are you satisfied with the life you are living, and would you choose to live the same life over again in an afterlife were one to exist?*

*philosopher of receptivity*

# Lao Tzu

571 BCE CHINA    5ᵗʰ CENTURY BCE CHINA

## *Attain Complete Emptiness Hold Fast to Stillness*

Lao Tzu is a philosopher of receptivity. He is the founder of Taoism and teacher of the Tao. "Tao" means way or path in Chinese. For Lao Tzu, the way consists in effortless and spontaneous action in harmony with nature. In Taoist cosmology, humans are born from nothing and return to nothing. This nothing is the Tao. The Tao is the life-force that flows through everything: past, present, and future. It allows each thing to become itself and thrive according to its own nature. The Tao cannot really be named, as it expands beyond anything that the mind can conceptualize. This is why it is characterized by Lao Tzu as a mystery, as nothing, as the empty. The Tao unfolds in nature and human existence without limit. "Something unformed and complete, Before heaven and earth were born, Solitary and silent, Stands alone and unchanging, Pervading all things without limit. It is like the mother of all under heaven, But I don't know its name—Better to call it Tao. Better call it great."[12]

Through his observations of nature and harmonious communities, Lao Tzu learned that things unfold best when they are left alone. Taoism builds on this insight. Things grow, flourish, and decline in keeping with their own way of being in the Tao. Our lives unfold naturally when we follow our instincts instead of impeding nature. Freed from social conventions and expectations, and from the willful interference that thwarts spontaneity, we find harmony with the world and discover that we are perfect just the way we are. Simplicity and non-action are the way of the Tao. "Act and you ruin it. Grasp and you lose it. Therefore the Sage does not act [*wu wei*] and so does not ruin, does not grasp, and so does not lose."[13]

Taoists believe that life is simple and that nature knows best. We swim against the current when we fight the flow of nature and seek to control or force things. By overthinking we make things complex. Just as our hearts beat naturally before we interrupt them by concentrating on their rhythm, so our lives unfold naturally when they are not stifled by self-consciousness, doubt, dwelling on the past, or worrying about the future. This is why Lao Tzu asks us to forget what we think we know and follow the path of simplicity. "In pursuit of knowledge, every day something is added. In the practice of the Tao, every day something is dropped. Less and less do you need to force things, until finally you arrive at non-action. When nothing is done, nothing is left undone. True mastery can be gained by letting things go their own way. It can't be gained by interfering."[14]

Taoists believe it is vanity to think we are able to understand the vastness of the world. When we define things or desire things to turn out a certain way we imprison the world and confine our natures. The world and universe are without boundaries. They are bound only by the relationships that exist among living beings and between things. The Tao is this between that holds everything together. Yet the Tao does not determine anything.

Rather, it yields to things so that they may reveal themselves as they are, each according to their own inner momentum. This is why the Tao cannot be named: it is empty, nothing, coming into existence only in the relationships that it holds together and makes possible. "Tao is empty—Its use is never exhausted. Bottomless—The origin of all things."[15]

Just as the silence between musical notes is integral to the integrity of the sound, so too the nothing of the Tao holds together and supports the integrity of life. Lao Tzu provides the images of a wheel, a pot, and a room to point to the nature of the Tao as the empty nothing. A pot may be used as a vessel for flowers, or as a spittoon to spit out tobacco. If it holds wine in a church, it is used for spiritual libations. If it is filled with beans on a stove, it serves as a cooking utensil to provide nourishment. The pot itself remains empty, but its meaning and use differ according to how the empty space is filled. "Thirty spokes join one hub. The wheel's use comes from emptiness. Clay is fired to make a pot. The pot's use comes from emptiness. Windows and doors are cut to make room. The room's use comes from emptiness."[16] Likewise, our ability to receive the Tao lies in our capacity to remain empty and allow ourselves to be filled by its mystery. Inner tranquility is a sign that we are in harmony with the Tao. "No desire is serenity, and the world settles itself."[17]

The Tao is empty. It is nothing; as such it has no limits. Boundaries close off things. Completion fixes things unnaturally and causes pain. When we think a possibility or a relationship is closed off, we tend to feel stuck, defeated and sad. We believe we have lost an opportunity or missed a moment. But these feelings are based in a misunderstanding of the Tao. Loss does not exist because there is no completion. The Tao does not lose or gain anything. It is forever unfolding. When we stop complicating our lives we can find joy in the routines of our everyday lives. "Things grow and grow, but each goes back to its root.

Going back to the root is stillness. This means returning to what is. Returning to what is means going back to the ordinary. Understanding the ordinary: is Enlightenment."[18]

Lao Tzu believes that all conflict is self-created. Human will, desire, and ambition impede the natural flow of the Tao. When we like this or that thing, we separate it from the whole and put it in opposition against that which we dislike. When we desire this or that outcome and set it off from other outcomes, we break the unity of life. Distinctions do not belong to the Tao. The Taoist symbol of yin and yang represents the harmony of opposites in the ever-changing cycles of nature that belong to the Tao.

Things unfold perfectly when they are left to follow their own natural course. This is why Lao Tzu promotes the principle of *wu wei,* or non-action, literally, doing without doing. *Wu wei* accomplishes by doing nothing. In doing without doing we respond to the world spontaneously and are receptive to all things. Doing without doing we open ourselves up to the wonder of the universe and let ourselves be impressed by the world and others. This openness occurs in passivity and stillness. Through unforced, unrehearsed, and instinctive actions, we become one with the Tao. Attuned to the Tao in *wu wei,* we allow everything to come together and fall apart according to its own inner rhythm and vital energies—its *ch'i.* "Practice not-doing, and everything will fall into place."[19]

Like a good swimmer who forgets the water, we flow with the currents of life in effortless action that is spontaneous and free. When we are too invested in something we create an unnatural situation and lose our way. We work against the grain, opposing the Tao. In tune with nature we flow with the Tao in creative interdependence with others and the world. In the stillness of *wu wei* we come into the realization that doing nothing and remaining silent are where our power lies. "The softest thing in the world, rides roughshod over the strongest."[20]

Yet, abiding in the stillness and silence of *wu wei* paradoxically takes practice. By doing nothing in *wu wei*, we are doing something—holding ourselves back from controlling mindsets and concerns with the noise of everyday life to create a space to let the world and others show themselves as they are. By remaining open and empty in stillness and silence we become receptive, rather than reactive, and act spontaneously to the world and others around us. "Attain complete emptiness, hold fast to stillness."[21] Freed from the impositions of our anxieties and desires we let others simply be. In stillness, genuine listening and deep connection are possible.

We are in harmony with ourselves and the world when we trust in the rhythms of nature. Nevertheless, Taoism is not a science or a religion but an art of living. Once we have benefited from its lessons, Lao Tzu asks us to discard his words, for they too are impediments to living a simple life. As his follower Chuang Tzu explains: "A trap is for fish: when you've got the fish, you can forget the trap. A snare is for rabbits: when you've got the rabbit, you can forget the snare. Words are for meaning: when you've got the meaning, you can forget the words. Where can I find someone who's forgotten words so I can have a word with him?"[22]

Tao- Mysterious, flows, nothing, full, beyond rational comprehension

you have to become empty in order to be fulled with the Tao

# APPLYING LAO TZU'S PHILOSOPHY

Lao Tzu asks you to trust your instincts and live in harmony with nature. By intuitively navigating life, you can be receptive to the infinite possibilities of the Tao. The world is mysterious and beyond your capacity for understanding. To walk the way of the Tao is to become part of the mystery and align yourself with its power. Attuned to the Tao, you understand that everything is perfect just as it is and that you are part of this perfection. Clear your mind so it can act as a mirror reflecting things in their simplicity, each according to its own inner nature. This is only possible when you step back from the noise that fogs the mirror of a clear mind and allow things to fall naturally into place. Stop overly reflecting on your life and free yourself from the confines of self-consciousness so that you can live without inhibitions. You do not have to fit into any mold. The Tao is formless and will shape itself to suit your life when you meet it by living spontaneously. When your mind is empty it serves as the soil for something new and unknown to emerge.

Let go of unimportant matters to make room for deeper sources of meaning. The more you think you know, the more you try to control your life, the less you allow the world and others to show themselves as they are and offer you their gifts. Do without doing and see without seeing in the stillness and silence of *wu wei*. At first you may experience this stillness as boredom or anxiety, lacking the drama of a complicated life. Work through this anxiety by refraining from judgment and criticism and just let things be. The ordinary contains the mystery. Constantly grappling with your decisions or trying too hard at something are signs that what you are doing may not be right for you. In trying to control things or other people you distort the Tao and create an unnatural situation. Just as when you begin to concentrate on your walking, it becomes forced and out of rhythm, so too when you limit the Tao you lose your way and fail to see the path clearly. Impeding the flow of nature, you promote obstruction instead of possibility. Letting go just a little has the potential to open up endless possibilities. Each pause is an opportunity for you to connect to silence and stillness and allow yourself to abide in the mystery of the Tao. Live simply and go through life with ease. You are on the right course when you lose yourself in what you are doing to become part of a natural flow with the Tao.

## QUESTIONS FOR CONSIDERATION

- *Do you allow yourself to live spontaneously?*

- *Do you trust your instincts?*

- *Are you able to accept what the world has to offer by remaining open to mystery and unknown possibilities?*

- *What does your life look like when you allow it to unfold more slowly and naturally in harmony with others and the world?*

- *Are parts of your life rehearsed or contrived?*

- *In what ways might you be making your life unnecessarily complicated instead of living in harmony with yourself?*

- *Do you obsess about problems or try to control situations that you are better off simply accepting?*

- *Do you allow others to express themselves by being still and leaving space for silence?*

- *What relationships and activities unfold easily for you?*

- *When are you in an experience of flow—fully embodied and at one with your surroundings—and what you are doing when this experience occurs?*

# Siddhartha Gautama (Buddha)

566 BCE INDIA    486 BCE INDIA

## *Homeless One Is Ever At Home*
## *Egoless One Is Ever Full*

Siddhartha Gautama (the Buddha) is a philosopher of impermanence. He believes that suffering, due to our inability to accept impermanence, is at the root of our existence. This is his first noble truth: life is suffering (*dukkha* in Sanskrit). His second, third, and fourth noble truths teach us the causes of suffering and how to end it. The Buddha wants us to understand that suffering is rooted in attachment. This is his second noble truth. The world is always changing. Situations and people come and go; our feelings and desires come and go. Nothing remains the same. When we realize that the nature of existence is impermanence, that old age, illness, death, and the loss of loved ones are inevitable, then we are more able to embrace the wisdom of non-attachment—the Buddha's third noble truth.

Thus, the Buddha teaches that suffering stems from our false beliefs about the nature of reality and the self. We desire stability and security, and fear loss and change. Yet the world is impermanent, and we are therefore bound to suffer through our attachments. "Selfish attachment brings suffering; selfish attachment brings fear. Be detached, and you will be free from suffering and fear."[23] We become attached to our ideas and to how we want things, others, and our selves to be. We grow attached to our homes, to our youth, to our jobs, to feeling happy, and suffer when these are no more. But we must learn that we cannot take hold of anything in a world whose nature consists in the cycles of birth and death (*samsara* in Sanskrit). Nothing is permanent: everything is always changing. This means that loss is inevitable—and with loss comes suffering. "Whatever is impermanent is *dukkha*."[24]

Once we understand the cause of suffering, we may begin to eradicate it. We do this through education to arrive at enlightenment. Buddhists tell the story of Kisa Gotami, who was overcome with grief after the loss of her only child. Crying out desperately with her desire to have her boy returned to her, she sought help from the Buddha. He promised to heal her pain if she could bring back a mustard seed from a home in which no one had died. Filled with hope, she went from door to door searching in vain. There was not a home in the land that did not suffer the loss of a loved one. She then came to understand the Buddha's teachings on suffering and impermanence, and the wisdom of compassion and non-attachment.

The Buddha teaches that the suffering we feel has an origin: it is rooted in desire and attachment. We suffer because we do not see reality as it is, but as we desire it to be. We want to have control over our lives, but planning for the future is rooted in ignorance of the changing natures of the world and the self. Consequently, we don't encounter reality but rather illusion. We take illusion to be reality through the screen of our perceptions and desires. As the Buddha explains, "To be attached to one thing (to a certain view) and to look down upon other things (views) as inferior—this the wise men call a fetter."[25]

Chief among our attachments is our clinging to the self, or our egos. The Buddha aims to free us from the fetters of the self so that we may eradicate desire and attachment. "All states are without self; those who realize this are freed from suffering. This is the path that leads to pure wisdom."[26] The self is an illusion, a fabrication of the mind. It is the basis of all egoism, selfishness, craving, and pride. The bundle of thoughts, memories, fears, desires, and anxieties that characterize what we call a self are not enduring. There is no substance upon which these moments attach: no thinker behind the thoughts, feeler behind the emotions, or doer behind the deeds. For the Buddha, suffering ceases as soon as the sufferer is no more. By doing away with the self who suffers, we do away with suffering. "Mere suffering exists, but no sufferer is found. The deeds are, but no doer is found."[27] By clinging to nothing, we lose nothing—this is the Buddha's cure to end suffering. "Him I call a Brahmin who has turned his back upon himself. Homeless, he is ever at home; egoless, he is ever full."[28]

Empty and free of ego, we release ourselves from attachments to live in the present, like mirrors that reflect reality and allow the world to shine forth moment by moment. The following parable, perhaps Taoist in origin, is used frequently in Buddhism to illustrate the wisdom of non-attachment. A farmer's horse ran away from him. His neighbors came to console him saying, "Too bad, too bad." The farmer responded, "Maybe." The next day the horse returned, bringing with him seven wild horses. "Oh, how lucky you are!" his neighbors exclaimed. "Maybe," the farmer responded. On the following day, the farmer's son tried to ride one of the new horses and was thrown off, breaking his leg. "How awful!" cried the neighbors. "Maybe," the farmer replied. The next day, soldiers came to conscript the young men of the village into the army, but the farmer's son wasn't taken because of his broken leg. "How wonderful for you!" the neighbors said. "Maybe," responded the farmer.[29]

This parable illustrates that what we may think is good or bad has no basis in reality. It is an illusion to think that we can judge things in isolation from the whole. Wisely, the farmer does not presume to know what the world has in store for him, nor does he presume to judge what the best course of events is for his life. He does not think that his limited mind can understand the vast workings of the world. Setting himself free from judgment, ego, and attachment, the farmer does not immediately react to events but allows space for meaning to emerge, and for things to happen as they do. We are not supposed to understand everything. The causes and relations we string together to explain the world do not reflect reality but the workings of our overactive minds. Through the wisdom of non-attachment, we allow the world to be as it is, and ourselves to greet things as they come.

Nothing is stable and nothing remains the same: not even the self that suffers remains the same. The Buddha teaches us that our minds are fixed by habits that we have acquired throughout our lives. Thoughts and sensations arise out of conditions, and they come and go with these certain conditions. To get attached to our thoughts, feelings, or sensations is rooted in a lack of knowledge regarding impermanence. Emotions or anxieties can be cast aside just as easily as they arise. Our task is to give them a space to appear and then allow them to disappear. Letting go of our attachments is the work of meditation, in which we practice how to discipline our minds and replace selfish desire and craving with universal love, compassion and kindness. "Meditation brings wisdom; lack of meditation leaves ignorance."[30]

Meditation aims to soften the rigid shapes of our minds and make them pliable again. In meditation, we observe arising thoughts without judgment, criticism, or discrimination, while focusing on our breath to help clear the mind. As thoughts pass by, we begin to embrace the idea of change. We also learn to reorient our minds from a cluttered and defensive state to one that is calm and responsive. Through the work of disciplining our minds we empty the mind of its baggage so that we may live fully in the present, free of fear and worry for the future. "As an archer aims his arrows, the wise aim their restless thoughts, hard to aim, hard to restrain."[31]

Sitting in meditation under the Bodhi Tree in Bodh Gaya, Siddhartha (the Buddha) experienced this liberation from the self. He was born a prince in what is now Nepal; an astrologer revealed to his father that Siddhartha would grow to be either a great king or a spiritual teacher. To ensure his son would follow in his footsteps, the King kept him within palace grounds and showered him with luxuries and amusements of all kinds. Siddhartha was shielded from all suffering and received all that he desired. Eventually, however, he grew restless and wanted to go beyond the palace walls. Remembering the astrologer's prophecy, his father had the streets cleared of the poor, sick, and hungry.

As he made his way through the city, Siddhartha was greeted by cheering crowds. Yet he slowly began to see signs of illness and old age. Toward the end of his journey he saw a corpse on the side of the road and asked why the body was lying there. His charioteer explained that death had come for the man, and that it would come for everyone regardless of wealth or age. Deeply troubled by the suffering he had encountered, the Buddha surrendered his title and privileges and left the palace in search of answers. After years of seeking, he retreated into meditation under the Bodhi tree and soon arrived at enlightenment, or Nirvana. No longer sleepwalking through life, Siddhartha declared: "I am awake." This is the literal meaning of the word "Buddha": it is from the Sanskrit root *budh*, "to wake up."[32]

When we grasp the nature of impermanence and suffering, we are able to feel compassion for all sentient beings who suffer like us. For the Buddha, enlightenment lies in our compassionate understanding of the fragility and temporary nature of all living beings. However, while the Buddha teaches non-attachment to a self or ego, this does not equate to a release from having to be responsible for our thoughts and actions. For the Buddha, we are not our thoughts, but our thoughts do filter reality and shape our perceptions. They determine the situations within which we find ourselves, and they create habits that lock us into patterns of thought that we have less and less control over with every succeeding repetition. This is the Law of Karma, which means "action" or "deed" in Sanskrit.

According to the Law of Karma, all thoughts and actions are conditioned by previous thoughts and actions and lay the foundation for subsequent thoughts and actions of the same kind. "Our life is shaped by our mind; we become what we think. Suffering follows an evil thought as the wheels of a cart follow the oxen that draw it. Our life is shaped by our mind; we become what we think. Joy follows a pure thought like a shadow that never leaves."[33] Negative thoughts set the course for even more negativity, while positive thoughts create a force for more positivity and good karma. "Let no one think lightly of evil and say to himself, 'Sorrow will not come to me.' Little by little a person becomes evil, as a water pot is filled by drops of water. Let no one think lightly of good and say to himself, 'Joy will not come to me.' Little by little a person becomes good, as a water pot is filled by drops of water."[34] Indeed, Buddhists believe that we come into the world with an inherited baggage of lifetimes of causal connections between our thoughts and actions—this is the root of the Buddhist theory of reincarnation.

When we understand the origins of suffering in attachment and the wisdom of non-attachment, we move from action governed by habit to action guided by the principles put forth in the Buddha's "eightfold path." This is his fourth noble truth. The eight principles of the eightfold path are right understanding, right thought, right speech, right action, right livelihood, right effort, right mindfulness, and right concentration. At the heart of all these principles lies compassion. The Buddha asks us to conquer unkindness through kindness. He asks us to discipline our minds and stay upright in our thoughts and actions. This is how we create good karma. "Whatever is positive, what benefits others, what conduces to kindness or peace of mind, those states of mind lead to progress; give them full attention. Whatever is negative, whatever is self-centered, what feeds malicious thoughts or stirs up the mind, those states of mind draw one downward; turn your attention away."[35]

The Buddha provides us with tools that aid in awakening and enlightenment. Enlightenment itself, however, cannot be taught, as it transcends language and all attempts by the mind to explain it. Only in retrospect, from the position of already having attained enlightenment, can we fully grasp its meaning. Until then, enlightenment must be sought on a principle of faith, fostered by the right training and education on the nature of impermanence. In the parable of the raft, the Buddha compares his teachings to a raft carrying us toward compassion, wisdom, tranquility, and enlightenment. But we must not hold onto these teachings dogmatically. Attachment, even attachment to Buddhist doctrine, produces suffering. Once enlightenment is attained, the Buddha asks us to discard the path: "In the same manner . . . I have taught a doctrine similar to a raft—it is for crossing over, and not for carrying."[36] Through the correct understanding of the nature of impermanence and non-attachment backed by right action, effort, and compassion, suffering can be overcome and enlightenment attained.

# APPLYING BUDDHA'S PHILOSOPHY

The Buddha wants you to understand the nature of suffering so that you may free yourself from it. Understand the nature of imperma- nence and release yourself from suffering through non-attachment. Learn how to live free of desires and selfish cravings that are rooted in your attachment to your ego. Suffering ceases when the self that suffers is no more. Do not cling to your thoughts: let them come and go with the changing situations that give rise to them. If you grab hold of nothing, you will have nothing to lose. Observe the movements of your thoughts, feelings, hopes, and fears and ask what patterns they follow. These patterns are born of habit. Do not cling to them. Thoughts and feelings are impermanent: they cause suffering only when you identify with them and attach them to the illusion of a stable and unchanging self. Work to empty yourself of your ego and respond to situations as they arise instead of through the lens of your ego with all its fears and desires.

When you free yourself from the bondage of self-absorption, you will begin to see things more clearly as they are and less as you want them to be. This will require work. Paths worn by habit are difficult to overcome. Your thoughts and actions are conditioned by your previous thoughts and actions and go on to condition your future thoughts and actions. This is the Law of Karma. You can change your karmic legacy and reprogram your thoughts, however. Practice mindfulness. Create positive karma by viewing, experiencing, and acting in the world with kindness. Compassion is your true nature. Free yourself from thoughts and actions that create habits that hin- der your path toward enlightenment. Refrain from hateful speech and gossip: instead, direct your attention toward creating universal good will and compassion. The way you approach the world and others determines the responses you will get. If you lead with com- passion, you will be greeted in kind. Be vigilant over your thoughts and actions and train them through mental and physical discipline. Follow the Buddha's eightfold path to enlightenment.

# QUESTIONS FOR CONSIDERATION

- *Are there any thoughts or actions that you may be clinging to?*

- *How might your attachments be connected to your suffering?*

- *What ideas and desires do you identify with to create the illusion of a consistent self?*

- *What are your thoughts on nonattachment?*

- *What does impermanence mean to you?*

- *Are you able to observe your thoughts and identify their patterns?*

- *Do you believe that it is possible to let your thoughts, feelings, and emotions pass by, or to let them visit for a while and then send them on their way?*

- *Can you imagine clearing your mind and emptying yourself of ego, cravings, and desires?*

- *Do you believe that your current actions and thoughts sow the seeds for future thoughts and actions of the same kind?*

- *Are you able to take a couple of minutes each day to observe your breath and check in with yourself in peace and solitude?*

- *What does the idea of compassion mean to you, and how would your life be different if you exercised more compassion?*

# Confucius

551 BCE CHINA    449 BCE CHINA

## *Acquire Roots Through Ritual and Tradition*

Kongzi is a philosopher of tradition. He is also popularly known by his Latinized name, Confucius. He teaches us that ritual and tradition bestow us with roots. These roots allow us to flourish and to understand ourselves and our places within the world. For Confucius, there are no random facts about our lives. Everything is determined by fate, which reflects a grand universal order that is both necessary and good. The time and place of our births, the families into which we are born, and the historical contexts within which we find ourselves all have cosmic and moral meaning for Confucius. He disagrees with thinkers who discard these things as not having been chosen, and who promote self-fashioning based on whim and fancy. For Confucius, life is not a matter of creating or discovering meaning but of understanding our roles within the nexus of traditions and rituals belonging to our communities. By understanding ourselves within a tradition—as part of a family, a culture, and ultimately humanity—we avoid the pitfalls of anxiety and isolation that come with creating a self out of nothing. As Confucius says, "Someone who is broadly learned with regard to culture, and whose conduct is restrained by the rites, can be counted upon to not go astray."[37]

Confucius wants us to know where we come from so that we are more confident in where we are going. Years of ritual practice have determined the suitable modes of conduct for each situation. He thinks there is no need to reinvent the wheel. Looking back to our past, we can find worthy models to guide our practices and transform our lives. Adapting roles and making them our own is how Confucius thinks we can circumvent the uncertainty of random choices that are not anchored by history. Drawing on the strength of our ancestors, we plant our feet in the firm soil of the past. To live according to ritual is to grasp of ourselves as belonging to a cultural heritage and social world. By standing on the pillars of our heritage, we become part of something bigger than ourselves. Internal harmony lies in being part of a whole and knowing our place there.

Confucius asks us to embrace our past rather than to invent or reinvent ourselves. He wants us to claim over our fates by taking up what is already ours. Creatively adopting and adapting traditions and rituals is one way to provide our lives with structure. Rituals are symbolic reminders of our traditional beliefs: they help us to navigate the world and find deeper meaning in our lives. Traditions provide a historical basis for understanding who we are and how we should act in community with others. Without some sort of model upon which to pattern our lives, Confucius thinks there would be chaos within the self and the universe. Knowing where we fit in the grand scheme of things we can act with equanimity and confidence. "Very few people go astray who comport themselves with restraint."[38] For Confucius, every detail of life must be educated by ritual and performed in complete awareness, down to the simplest of things: how we eat, speak, dress, and even the degree of sincerity we feel toward each other. It was said, for example, that Confucius would never sing on a day that he had wept.

Through discipline and moral self-cultivation, Confucius teaches us to understand ourselves as members of a community united by traditions, upheld by rituals, and supported by a moral universe. In Confucius's worldview, the universe and society mirror each other. They are held together by the actions of individuals in relationship to others, beginning with those in the family and culminating in the love of humanity (*ren* in Chinese). When people act morally and formally according to societally prescribed roles, with sincerity and joy in their hearts, there is trust and love among people. Loyalty, respect, and honor reign, and the universe is in order. When we are led by self-interest or whims, chaos ensues. Stability is lost because we no longer have a historical basis for understanding who we are and how to act. Mistrust grows when we fail to act transparently according to expectations and customs that are designed for the good of humanity. Just as different musical notes complement each other and come together to create a harmony, so too we are all part of a harmony greater than ourselves. Through behavior governed by ritual modes of conduct, we transform our individual passions toward a love of humanity.

Confucius is perhaps the first thinker to have worked out such an enduring system of ethics—his system has set the moral tone and foundation for ethical education in China for thousands of years. Nevertheless, Confucius does not present himself as a philosopher, but as a historian entrusted with passing on the wisdom of ancient customs. There are no divine sources for Confucian practices, nor does Confucius refer to a transcendent God. Confucianism is not a religion, but a way of life like that introduced by his older contemporary Lao Tzu. Each introduced their own Tao, which means "way," into Chinese society. However, contrary to Lao Tzu's Tao, which is based in simplicity, the abandonment of social roles and rituals, and a return to nature, the Tao for Confucius lies in reflective and deliberate moral action in keeping with societal norms and ritual customs.

Confucius thinks that there are discoverable moral truths in the natural world. The order of the universe is reflected in the microcosm of the cultural and familial roles we inhabit. For Confucius, the universe cares about what we do because our actions have the power to alter its balance. Harmony prevails just so long as we act like a superior individual or *junzi*, often translated as "gentleman," who knows their place. He tells us that "One who does not understand fate lacks the means to become a *junzi*. One who does not understand ritual lacks the means to take his place."[39]

Confucius's main teachings are collected in the *Analects*, which contain fragments of conversations between Confucius and his followers. They describe many instructions on how to live a moral life. Confucius teaches us that honesty holds the universe together. Where there is dishonesty, words and deeds do not accord with reality, and there is chaos. He asks us to be humble and to know our abilities and limits. He asks us not to be afraid to admit our mistakes and to learn from them. "The Master said, 'To make a mistake and yet to not change your ways—this is what is called truly making a mistake.'"[40] We should always strive to remain high-minded: "The gentleman (*junzi*) understands higher things, whereas the petty person understands only the low."[41] We should not follow the multitude but judge for ourselves. We must also be fair. Reportedly, Confucius "would fish with a hook, but not with a net."[42]

Confucius asks us also not to allow greed or money to motivate us and implores us to act on the basis of virtue. He gives the example of a piece of jade that he wishes to sell. Yet he does not simply seek to sell it to the highest bidder but rather to the person who is most deserving of it. "I am just waiting for the right offer," he says.[43] Better than counting profits is a time spent cultivating virtues: "The gentleman understands rightness, whereas the petty person understands profit."[44] Perhaps the most well-known

Confucian teaching is the one that he and Jesus have in common. Confucius was the first to formulate a negative version of the principle of the Golden Rule: "Do not impose upon others what you yourself do not desire."[45]

All people are capable of being good. However, we are not born good but must cultivate morality within ourselves through education. If someone acts poorly, this is because of bad training, government, or upbringing. Confucius believes that "By nature people are similar; they diverge as the result of practice."[46] Good character is about knowing the proper action for each occasion. But it is not enough to simply know and act well. We must also feel a connection to our actions and find joy in the roles we perform. Above all, Confucius values sincerity. He discourages action that is perfunctory and routine rather than heartfelt, saying: "One who knows it is not the equal of one who loves it, and one who loves it is not the equal of one who takes joy in it."[47] Duty, restraint, love of humanity, and sincerity are what characterize a *junzi*: "The gentleman takes rightness as his substance, puts it into practice by means of ritual, gives it expression through modesty, and perfects it by being trustworthy. Now that is a gentleman!"[48]

For Confucius, we all have a role to play within the social order and are responsible for playing our roles well: "Let the lord be a true lord, the ministers true ministers, the fathers true fathers, and the sons true sons."[49] Children must respect their parents and elders, as this is their filial duty. Parents and elders must act and be worthy of respect. To measure filial devotion, Confucius instructs us to observe how someone acts after their parents have died. If they keep to their parents' teachings then, they have fulfilled their filial love and duty. Most importantly, leaders must be benevolent and rule in service to their citizens. The goodness of our leaders is reflected in the functioning of our society. If there is order and harmony among the people, then the leader is benevolent. When the rule of force is in place, then a leader has failed. Confucius believes that the citizenry mirrors the moral character of their leader, and that the leader sets the standard of behavior for society.

Confucius lived during a time of great conflict and division in China, known as the Spring and Autumn period. China had consisted of numerous kingdoms engaged in generations-long battles which crippled the social order. Although there was total war, with each region vying for power, Confucius could see the coming unification of China. He looked to lessons from the past, believing that through tradition and ritual he could unify his society and avoid the chaos that was threatening to engulf it. He believed that a people who knew their history, read classical texts, and were loyal to ancient ways would be able to unite and hold their society together. Confucius traveled from state to state in search of a leader who would put his moral teachings into practice. He ultimately failed to find a patron ruler who would lead through virtue instead of force and power.

Eventually Confucius went into exile. He died upon his return to his home state believing he had made no lasting impact on Chinese society. Indeed, Chinese thinkers after Confucius criticized him for privileging familial relations and especially for encouraging spending on the pomp of ceremony instead of directing public monies toward social services and education for the needy. But these critics failed to recognize Confucius's wisdom. Ceremony, tradition, and ritual did the work of securing a united Chinese culture that provided a strong sense of national identity. They continue to provide the glue that binds us to others in our communities, both past and present, while setting a course for the future.

# APPLYING CONFUCIUS' PHILOSOPHY

Confucius wants you to give order and meaning to your life by understanding yourself within the history of a tradition. Avoid the anxiety that comes from aimlessly trying to find yourself. Draw from the strength of your ancestors; they have a lot to teach you. Take up threads from your past and weave them into your everyday life. There is always something in your past that you can make your own, something that you may want to cultivate, transform, or refine. Embracing a past that gives meaning to your present through ritual practice keeps you stable in trying times, when the ground may seem to shift beneath your feet. Revitalize your traditions and root yourself in the firm soil of the past. Knowing who you are within a narrative history gives you more confidence in where you are going, because you know where you are coming from.

Step outside of your individual concerns and join with others through ritual and tradition. Understand your life within the context of family and community. In community you can deepen your relationships with others. Showing respect for your elders and honoring the ways of the past form the foundation for ethical living. Participate in ceremonies to mark important passages of life, even if the time and cost is inconvenient. These ceremonies create memories and give meaning to life's different phases. Comport yourself with honor, dignity, and nobility in all situations. Take your roles seriously. If you are a parent, then discipline, love, and teach as a parent. If you are a leader, then lead. Roles and rituals are there to establish order and provide structure. By adhering to patterns of principled and consistent actions, you gain mastery over yourself and stability in your relationships.

# QUESTIONS FOR CONSIDERATION

- *What rituals and traditions do you practice to give order and meaning to your life?*

- *What elements in your life provide you with roots?*

- *Do you recognize yourself within a historical framework?*

- *Are there any traditions and rituals from your upbringing that you have taken up, or would like to incorporate into your life?*

- *Are there any traditions and rituals that you have learned about that you would like to adopt?*

- *Do you belong to a community, or is there a community you wish to join on the merits of its rituals and practices?*

- *Do you approach the roles you play in life with sincerity, or do you simply go through the motions?*

- *Are there any customs that you would like to pass down to the next generation?*

- *How do you address your feelings of rootlessness?*

- *What can you learn by drawing from your ancestors?*

# Aristotle

385 BCE GREECE    322 BCE GREECE

## *Character Is Your Guide to Virtues*

Aristotle is a philosopher of character. He teaches us how to flourish by being the best we can be relative to our own innate abilities. Aristotle's primary concern is character development. While he does not think we are born with any particular character traits, he does think we each have unique tendencies that dispose us toward some actions over others. Flourishing occurs when we find a harmony between our innate tendencies and the exercise of virtues such as honesty, courage, and generosity. He calls this balance between virtues and our dispositions our "mean." It is arrived at through good and rational judgment rooted in self-knowledge and an awareness of doing the right thing. For Aristotle, happiness is attained by judging well, and doing so consistently throughout our lifetimes. Consistent and virtuous action is the foundation of a strong character. "It follows, then, that the happy person has the stability we are looking for and keeps the character he has throughout his life."[50]

Aristotle takes as given that to act virtuously is to live well, be happy, and flourish. "The belief that the happy person lives well and does well also agrees with our account, since we have virtually said that the end is a sort of living well and doing well."[51] We flourish when we achieve pleasure by acting virtuously, and when we feel at home in our actions. This home is our character (*ethos* in Ancient Greek), which is the root of the term "ethics." Our characters are the place where we customarily dwell, where we feel most at home in our actions and in our lives. The aim, for Aristotle, is to develop an *ethos* where we experience pleasure in doing the right thing. Acting virtuously on the basis of having found our means, we know how to judge and act with the right measure to reach an equilibrium in our souls and a harmony with those around us.

Aristotle shows us that there is an art to knowing how and when to act, and that this art is the mark of a character that has found its center, its mean. Well-being is not attained by turning against our natures but by using our reason to strike the right balance between our dispositions and virtuous action. Finding our balance is a long-term exercise in learning how to find pleasure in doing the right thing by showing good judgment. This good judgment is what Aristotle calls *phronesis*. When our emotions, actions, and thoughts are aligned with our better judgement in *phronesis*, we flourish and are happy. *Eudaimonia* is the Ancient Greek term for happiness. It is an activity of the soul and the goal of human life. *Eudaimonia* differs from the modern understanding of happiness, however, which usually pertains to a state of mind or experience of pleasure. It is perhaps better translated as well-being or flourishing. *Eudaimonia* takes a long-term view of happiness, considering the duration of a life lived well in accordance with the virtues. Most importantly, *eudaimonia* is a skill to be cultivated. Pleasure is a part of *eudaimonia*, but it is the consequence of our well-being and flourishing, not its cause.

For Aristotle, the happy person does not have to deny their pleasure but derives it from doing the right thing and acting virtuously. If we are happy when we are pursuing what is good for us, then we will live a flourishing life. We flourish when we exercise good judgement, know why we act as we do, and act consistently out of a disposition that has found its center. Aristotle asks us to gauge how much work our characters need by how balanced we feel in our lives and by whether we are thriving or stagnating. If we are happy, then we feel repose in our actions, and are free from doubt, conflict, guilt, and remorse. Trusting ourselves to navigate all sorts of situations correctly is the mark of a good character.

Like his mentor Plato, Aristotle examines what it means to live a good life. However, unlike Plato, Aristotle does not search for general truths about the nature of the good, but rather asks how to make people good. As an empirical thinker, Aristotle models his idea of what it means to live a good life on those in his community who are worthy of admiration and imitation. Nevertheless, Aristotle recognizes that no two situations are exactly alike, just as no two people are alike. He therefore does not think it is possible to introduce universal principles for virtuous behavior. There is no one standard for ethical behavior in Aristotle's model: his is a virtue ethics rooted in character and the proper use of rational judgement.

Aristotle asks us to work on our characters as we would commit to learning a new language. Instead of prescribing guidelines for how to act, he asks us to know ourselves and find our mean, or comfort zone, by reading a situation and reading ourselves in different situations. A mean is a center-point or balance between two extremes regarding a virtue. We find our means in relation to virtues by seeking a balance between excessive be-havior and deficient behavior. Reacting to a situation with too much anger is a sign of a bad temper or extreme righteousness.

Having too little anger or outrage is a sign of a meek character, someone who does not stand firm on anything. But what it is to be too angry may not be the same for one person as for another.

The work of character development is therefore not an easy task, as it requires a good deal of self-knowledge, practice, and habitual training. "So also about getting angry, or giving or spending money, is easy and everyone can do it," Aristotle writes, "but doing it to the right person, in the right amount, at the right time, for the right end, and in the right way is no longer easy, nor can everyone do it. Hence doing things well is rare, praiseworthy, and fine."[52] About courage, Aristotle has this to say: "For if, for instance, someone avoids and is afraid of everything, standing firm against nothing, he becomes cowardly; if he is afraid of nothing at all and goes to face everything, he becomes rash. Similarly, if he gratifies himself with every pleasure and abstains from none, he becomes intemperate, if he avoids them all, as boors do, he becomes some sort of insensible person. Temperance and bravery, then, are ruined by excess and deficiency, but preserved by the mean."[53]

When we find our means, we may be said to be prudent and temperate. We act consistently and find pleasure in doing the right thing. Nevertheless, Aristotle acknowledges that sometimes we act against our better judgment by getting carried away by our emotions, failing to deliberate wisely, or failing to keep to the conclusions of our deliberations. We may know that the best action to take is to study for an upcoming exam, yet choose to go out with friends instead. Knowing the right thing to do but acting against our well-being is what Aristotle calls "incontinence" (*akrasia* in Greek). Incontinent people are filled with remorse and regret because they do not judge well and are unable to support their actions with reasons. They act against their better judgement because they have a weak will. Plagued by self-doubt, a person of bad character lacks consistency. They act one way on one day and a different way another day. Self-destructive behavior is rooted in a lack of measure, in a failure to find the balance between acting in excess or not doing enough.

A virtuous person, on the other hand, has the capacity to accept the principles that they present to themselves by their judgments. For Aristotle it is very important to have our actions be guided by principles that create habits that support good behavior. What we do now forms the dispositions that guide our future actions. Repeating bad behavior creates habits that produce a bad character. Likewise, by behaving well and doing well, we form good characters: "a person is a principle, begetting actions as he begets children."[54] But all is not lost for the incontinent person. They have the option to learn how to find pleasure in the right things through the development of good judgement. When we are in doubt, Aristotle asks us to develop our characters through imitation, by deliberating and choosing as a prudent person would choose in a particular circumstance.

Once we feel at home and are in harmony with ourselves, we can have harmonious relationships with others. What is ultimately assessed regarding the rightness of our deliberations is how our choices and actions impact others. For Aristotle, flourishing and well-being are realized in community with others. When deliberation is good, our choices have a salutary effect on others. Aristotle's ethics therefore constitute a study of how characters flourish and achieve well-being within a community. Indeed, his most fundamental belief is that we are social and political creatures by nature. We need the company of others for our well-being. Without friendship (*phila* in Greek), Aristotle thinks life would not be worth living. In the reciprocity of friendship, we show our characters and goodness. But here too, in friendship, we exercise practical wisdom and find the mean. Not all relationships are the same. Some relationships call for us to act with an eye toward mutual benefit, and others are aimed toward shared pleasure. The most noble relationship is based on goodwill and the mutual pursuit of living a good life.

Aristotle thinks that it is not wealth or competition but harmony in our relationships that makes us happy. He identifies three models of friendship: friendship of utility, friendship of pleasure, and friendship of the good. He asks us to properly judge the types of friendship we are keeping. Friendship of the good is the highest form of friendship because the friends pursue virtuous activity together, but Aristotle believes the other models are also significant. Friendship of utility is formed around mutual aid and benefit, and is often found in professional relationships. But it is easily dissolved once the friends are no longer useful to each other. Friendship of pleasure, like friendship of utility, is short lived. It is based on mutual pleasure and ceases once the relationship is no longer pleasurable. Friendship of the good, on the other hand, is not easily dissolvable. However, it is rare because it is difficult to find virtuous people and invest the time in getting to know one another. Aristotle thinks we are lucky to have one such friendship, maybe two at the most, during our lifetimes.

Friendship of the good is an enduring relationship between two mutually excellent characters who pursue the goal of a virtuous life together. Only those with self-love are capable of this form of friendship, which resembles a friendship with one's own self: "For friendship is community and we are related to our friend as we are related to ourselves[.]"[55] If we are filled with regret and are therefore unstable, we are unable to love ourselves well or be a good friend to another. We may surround ourselves with others, fearing to be alone with our memories, but these others are not friends. They are a means to an end—escaping from ourselves. Self-love, on the other hand, is rooted in a good character that has found harmony within itself and flourishes. When we are in harmony with ourselves, we seek out harmonious relationships with others that help us to be the best person we can be. This is why it is important to choose our friends wisely. Similar characters pursue common ends and goals. "Whatever someone regards as his being, or the end for which he chooses to be alive, that is the activity he wished to pursue in his friend's company."[56] Indeed, living well is reflected in the company we keep, in the very fabric of our relationships—starting with our own self relations. This is why Aristotle ultimately thinks that a good character is rooted in self-love: "one is a friend to himself most of all. Hence he should also love himself most of all."[57]

# APPLYING ARISTOTLE'S PHILOSOPHY

Aristotle wants you to know who you are so that you can flourish and act in ways that enhance your wellbeing. When you know who you are you can act with confidence to realize your full potential. This is the hallmark of a good character—feeling comfortable in your own skin such that your actions work to contribute to your wellbeing rather than thwart it. Your character is your *ethos*: the place where you feel at home in your actions. Learn how to act in the right way, toward the right things, at the right time, and with the right feelings. Find pleasure by acting virtuously. While you may get pleasure in actions that are not good for you, the difference between a strong and a weak character is that a strong character is able to steer themselves away from behavior that is harmful in the long run. They can do this because they have good judgment, or *phronesis*. Develop your capacity for *phronesis*. Choose appropriate goals and deliberate wisely about the means to attain your goals in a way that supports your ethical well-being.

Aristotle calls upon you to build a strong and consistent character. A bad character suffers from regret, remorse, pain, and doubt. If you experience pain and find yourself often out of sorts then you are not deliberating wisely or flourishing, and this is likely because your actions are out of balance with your character. Exercise moderation. Find your own unique balance, or mean, between acting in excess or acting too little. Know yourself and find your center to arrive at measured actions. Repeated actions become habits, and these habits are what form your character. If you engage in unvirtuous activities, you will habituate yourself toward vices and attract bad characters. Work to habituate yourself to following the right and virtuous course of action while being in harmony with your nature. Make good friendships that reflect the love you have for yourself.

# QUESTIONS FOR CONSIDERATION

- *Do you have a personal ethos, a strong character that guides your actions?*

- *Do you take pleasure in doing the right things that promote your ethical well-being?*

- *Do you ever feel out of balance and act against what you know is right?*

- *Are you able to find a balance between actions that are excessive and actions that are inadequate?*

- *Do you trust your judgements?*

- *Do you have confidence in your ability to say and do the right thing at any given time?*

- *Do others see you as consistent and reliable, having a sense of how you will act and what you will say in important matters?*

- *Do you temper what you know is good with your own personal dispositions, or do you try to act according to a standard model of what it means to be good?*

- *Do you have a sense of how best to judge different situations and what elements are important to factor into your decisions?*

- *What measures do you use to gauge your well-being?*

- *Do you confuse the nature of your relationships and sometimes give more or less than the relationship merits?*

- *Do you surround yourself with people who help you be the best you can be?*

# Epictetus

50 CE TURKEY    135 CE GREECE

## *People Are Disturbed Not by Things, but by Their Views of Things*

Epictetus is a philosopher of acceptance. He is a key thinker in the school of thought called Stoicism. Epictetus takes Socrates' lesson that a virtuous life is a good and happy life and turns it into a strict discipline backed by a deterministic model of the universe. Whereas Socrates defines himself as a midwife, helping others to give birth to wisdom he claims not to possess himself, Epictetus is more akin to a physician. He heals mental disturbances that sicken the soul by teaching us how to live in harmony with the universe. Everything happens for a reason, and if we understood the nature of the universe correctly we would wish for nothing to be different. Serenity and tranquility lie in acceptance of all that is and in understanding that the universe is good. Indeed, we do an injustice to ourselves and to the world when we are disappointed with life.

For Epictetus, the universe is fated and good and can be in no other way. That is why we must be thankful for everything that happens. We cannot change events in the past through our regret, or influence the future through our worry: the past and the future are out of our control. Epictetus asks us to stay focused only on what is within our control. Our thoughts, desires, emotions, and wills are in our control, while our bodies, property, reputations, and the opinions of others are out of our control. Through mental discipline and the wisdom to know and act only on what is within our control, we may overcome all hindrances.

Epictetus teaches us that our thoughts determine how we feel and experience the world. They shape our outlooks and wellbeing. If we change our thoughts, then we change our reality and how we feel about ourselves and the world. While we cannot always control what happens to us, we can control how we perceive and experience what happens to us. Illness may overcome our bodies, but we control how we respond to the illness. Suffering therefore does not come to us from the outside but is created by our own minds: "Men are disturbed, not by things, but by the principles and notions which they form concerning things. Death, for instance, is not terrible, else it would have appeared so to Socrates."[58]

We cause our own disturbances by trying to control things that are innately out of our control, like death, or other people's actions and opinions. Epictetus warns that it is foolhardy to be the cause of our own suffering. We must therefore exercise great care and discipline over our thoughts and direct them properly. The power is ours to avoid harm by refraining from negative and harmful thoughts and by not allowing others to disturb us. "Nothing can influence or control your thoughts, responses, impulses. Things may restrain your body, like illness, but what is most yourself is in your power."[59]

Serenity and calm are completely in our control. This is why Epictetus asks us to be vigilant over our thoughts and defend our minds as if an enemy lies in waiting. Just as we would not willingly hand our bodies over to someone who will cause us injury, so we must not recklessly hand our minds over to harmful thoughts or to the negativity brought about by others. He cautions us: "If a person gave your body to any stranger he met on his way, you would certainly be angry. And do you feel no shame in handing over your own mind to be confused and mystified by anyone who happens to verbally attack you?"[60] Again, Epictetus explains: "Just as in walking about you pay attention so as not to step on a nail or twist your foot, pay attention in the same way so as not to harm your ruling principle."[61]

Epictetus believes that we are part of something bigger than ourselves. All the world is interconnected and ordered according to a grand plan that is both rational and good. Our rational minds fit within the order of this physically determined universe. Freed from the influence of individual emotions and desires, we are asked to align our minds with the soul of the universe, where we will find contentment. In Stoic cosmology, everything happens for a reason and happens just as it should. It is therefore futile to go against our fates and seek to sever ourselves from the whole through unhappiness with our lot. This shows a lack not only of gratitude, but also of understanding our part in the universe.

Our fate is integrally bound to the destiny of the whole: the individual is part of the fabric of the universe. If we wish for any one thing in our lives to change, then everything must change. Destruction ensues. The past is past and the future is bound in uncertainty, bundled within a nexus of causes and effects that reach back incomprehensibly to the beginning of time. Our task is to understand that we belong to the universal order of things and are in good hands. Wishing for things to be as they are rather than as we would otherwise wish them to be is one of Epictetus's key teachings on happiness: "Do not seek to have events happen as you want them to, but instead want them to happen as they do happen, and your life will go well."[62]

We show gratitude by being satisfied with our lives. Failure is part of life. Sadness is part of life. But we control the magnitude and duration of how upset we get. It is in our power to see the world either in a way that makes us feel content, or in a way that disturbs our tranquility (*ataraxia* in Greek). We must always remember that what we think about events determines how we feel, and not the events themselves. No harm may come to us from outside unless we let it. We have the power to experience life free from anguish by directing our minds toward things that feed rather than starve our souls. By upholding affirming thoughts to avoid rather than to invite pain, we bring tranquility into our lives.

Epictetus provides us with many tools for living a more satisfied life, including ways to anticipate obstacles. When we go to a post office or another bureaucratic institution, we should not be upset if we encounter long lines, but rather expect the delays that such institutions tend to have. Likewise, we must understand that death is a natural and inevitable occurrence. When a neighbor dies, for example, we may feel empathy and sadness, but we accept that death happens. Yet when someone we love dies, or when death is at our own doorstep, we forget that loss belongs to the nature of the universe and is out of our control. Instead, we become despondent. On this matter, Epictetus does not mince words: "You are foolish if you want your children and your wife and your friends to live forever, since you are wanting things to be up to you that are not up to you, and things to be yours that are not yours . . . Whoever wants to be free, therefore, let him not want or avoid anything that is up to others. Otherwise, he will necessarily be a slave."[63]

Indeed, Epictetus was born a slave, but he teaches us that we are lords over our minds. It is not death itself that we find unbearable, as we are able to endure the death of a neighbor or those whom we do not know well. Rather, it is our thoughts and perceptions of death and our emotions surrounding the death of our loved ones that cause us pain. "Is the child or wife of another dead? There is no one who would not say, 'This is a human accident.' But if anyone's own child happens to die, it is presently, 'Alas, how wretched am I!'"[64] Reason can grasp this truth. And since our thoughts and emotions are in our control, Epictetus believes we are able to heal after we mourn, through the power of our thoughts.

We are travelers on this earth—alive now but soon to be gone. We must not waste the short time we have being dissatisfied with our lives. "While he gives it to you to possess, take care of it; but don't view it as your own, just as travelers view a hotel."[65] Others are in our lives for as long as the universe deems fit. We are here for only a certain length of time, and when this time runs out we must let go. Thus, Epictetus enjoins us to "Never say of anything, 'I have lost it'; but 'I have returned it.'"[66] We have the power to experience life in calm satisfaction by accepting our lives as they are and by being grateful for what we have. Serenity is our nature. We must therefore enjoy the lives we have and remind ourselves every morning to appreciate each day, as it may be our last. The great Stoic emperor Marcus Aurelius warns us not to be caught unawares: "'But I have not played my five acts, only three.' 'True, but in life three acts can be the whole play.'"[67]

Serenity and tranquility lie in the acceptance of things as they are. We are therefore asked to embrace the fate that the universe has uniquely spun for each of us and to value the precious time we have left. Epictetus writes that "Everything has two handles, the one by which it may be carried, the other by which it cannot."[68] We must choose the handle that carries and lifts us up high and not the handle that provides us with no support. Dissatisfaction is a sign that our minds have failed us before our bodies have: discontentment with life shows bad manners and a lack of virtue. Again, in the words of Aurelius, "Disgraceful if, in this life where your body does not fail, your soul should fail you first."[69]

Troubles are not found in the world but are self-created. Finding harmony in our lives, we learn to accept the gifts of the universe and are grateful for all that life has brought our way. In the modern Serenity Prayer, we hear the remnants of Epictetus' Stoicism: "God grant me the serenity to accept the things I cannot change, courage to change the things I can, and wisdom to know the difference."[70]

# APPLYING EPICTETUS' PHILOSOPHY

Epictetus asks you to entrust yourself and your wellbeing to the universe. There is nothing in this world that you cannot bear. Sometimes things may be hard, but don't get stuck in any one moment. Nothing remains the same: life has a way of making unexpected turns. Allow yourself to work with the universe, and doors will open for you. You are not being singled out by events that happen in your life. It is not life's circumstances that cause you suffering but how you view these circumstances. Keep your focus on the present and trust in the goodness of the universe to unfold as it will. Your experience is a necessary part of the fabric of the whole and fits into a larger plan that is unknown to you. Everything plays out exactly as it is destined to and can be in no other way than it is. No human action, no matter how great, can alter the past or determine the future. If you understand this, then you will not wish for anything to happen differently. Contentment is the best way to show gratitude for your life.

Keep your soul healthy and strong. Only you have the power to upset your tranquility, and so you can just as easily toss away all your troubles. Do not be the cause of your own disturbance by giving unreasonable attention to things that are out of your control. If you are anxious or sad, you are likely refusing to accept something that is beyond your control to change. Ask yourself if your worries are about things that are in your control or outside of your control, and work to let go of matters that are beyond your control. Other people's opinions of you are out of your control, but you can control how you let those opinions affect you. When you allow others to upset you, you don't realize that it is you and not them that are causing you distress. Do not relinquish control to others. Do not abdicate the care of yourself to others to manage. Your mind is your ruling power, and you control it. Nothing can harm you from the outside: all benefit and harm come from within. Do not harm yourself by thinking negative thoughts. The way you speak to yourself and the things that you say to yourself have the power to shape your life negatively or positively.

# QUESTIONS FOR CONSIDERATION

− *Do you believe that your thoughts influence how you feel and act and that you have the ability to change your life by changing your thoughts?*

− *Is there anything you are failing to accept that is beyond your power to change?*

− *Who or what is in control of your thoughts and emotions—you, or external events and people's opinions of you?*

− *Do your thoughts support you in living a contented life, or do they torment you with worry?*

− *Do you feed your mind with positive or negative thoughts?*

− *Are you able to focus your thoughts and actions on what is in your control or do you let people and events that are out of your control dictate how you feel?*

− *Are you able to let go of things that are outside of your control?*

− *How would your life be if you lived in the moment without being weighed down by past regrets or future worries?*

− *What would it feel like to believe you are part of a bigger plan, and that everything that happens in your life is destined to be and is perfect the way it is?*

− *Do you have a practice of mental and physical health that you follow with discipline?*

− *What is standing between you and serenity right now?*

# Augustine of Hippo

354 CE ALGERIA    430 CE ALGERIA

## *My Weight Is My Love By It I Am Carried Wherever I Am Carried*

Augustine is a philosopher of happiness. He writes about the soul's internal struggle to find happiness and calm—paradoxically, by way of unhappiness. He believes that each of us already knows what makes us happy. But whether it is by force of habit, self-destructive behavior, or inner conflict, transitioning to happiness will likely involve a struggle. Fortunately, when we are on the wrong path, our own dissatisfaction will serve as an engine guiding us to greater truth. In his *Confessions*, Augustine tells of his difficult journey to find the source of his happiness in God's love. His story is told from the perspective of having already converted to Christianity. His mother pleaded with him to take up religion, and from her he had knowledge of God's grace and rewards. He writes, "With you there is true rest and life untroubled. He who enters into you enters into the joy of his Lord, and he shall have no fear, and he shall possess his soul most happily in him who is the supreme good."[71] Yet Augustine teaches us that it is not enough to simply know. We must also believe in love and in our happiness: "believe so that you may understand."[72]

Augustine speaks to our feelings that something is missing or that something is not quite right. He yearned for happiness in God's love. But to know about God was not enough. It was necessary to love Him as well. Instead, Augustine initially directed his love outwardly, measuring his happiness by the standards of the material world. The pleasures of the flesh captivated him. Pride and vanity drove him. For Augustine, love has the power to transform us: what we love defines who we are. He writes: "My weight is my love. By it I am carried wherever I am carried."[73] If we love fame, wealth, power, and pleasure, our souls will become shallow. For a long time, Augustine loved these things, and they loved him back. By earthly measures, Augustine was primed for happiness. He had secured a prestigious position at the University of Milan and was on course to attain political power. He was popular, surrounded by friends, and had won distinction and celebrity as a Bishop and theologian. But he was not happy.

Augustine teaches us that we will be embraced in kind by that toward which we direct our love. He asks us to love and be loved by that which calls us to be happy and calm. While he had remembered the gifts that God bestows on those whom He loves, his soul was in conflict. Instead of loving God, Augustine was in love with his own undoing. "I neither willed it completely, nor did I refrain completely from willing it. Therefore, I was at war within myself, and I was laid waste by myself."[74] Yearning for happiness, Augustine was perplexed. How was it possible for him to desire happiness if he had never known it? How could he long for an overwhelming joy that would fill his soul with the security of being loved and cared for completely if he had never experienced such love? Augustine reasons that each of us already knows what makes us happy. Otherwise we would not know what to look for in our search for happiness, nor how to recognize it once we have found it. The unknown can never be the object of our desire. Augustine therefore concludes that

*Philosophy Wise*

happiness already lies complete within each of us, waiting for us to find it. Our happiness is always there, written in our hearts.

Augustine asks us to identify and examine what it is we truly desire. By delving deeply within and engaging with our inner demons and self-destructive habits, we can open ourselves to love and embrace the happiness that is innately within us. Through questioning, intense doubt, and soul-searching, Augustine opened himself to God's love. But to arrive at his happiness, he had to meet with his darkest, most shameful, and most painful moments. Augustine recounts the joy he had derived from his depravity in stealing a pear at the age of sixteen: "There was a pear tree close to our own vineyard, heavily laden with fruit, which was not tempting either for its color or for its flavor. Late one night—having prolonged our games in the streets until then, as our bad habit was—a group of young scoundrels, and I among them, went to shake and rob this tree. … Doing this pleased us all the more because it was forbidden. Such was my heart, O God, such was my heart—it was foul, and I loved it. I loved my own undoing. I loved my error—not that for which I erred but the error itself. A depraved soul, falling away from security in thee to destruction in itself, seeking nothing from the shameful deed but shame itself."[75]

Indeed, the deeper Augustine delved within, the more confused he became. Fear of the unknown kept sending him back to his accustomed habits. Augustine knew that happiness was to be found in the embrace of God's love, but he turned against God toward the pleasures of instant gratification, especially the pleasures of the flesh. Yet out of this confusion self-reflection was born. Augustine had become a question to himself. What he ultimately sought was an answer to the question: "Who am I?" "But do you, O Lord my God, graciously hear me, and turn your gaze upon me, and see me, and have mercy on me, and heal me. For in your sight I have become a riddle to myself, and that is my infirmity."[76]

Before Augustine, the soul was discussed vaguely, mostly re-garding where it came from, and where it was going to take us. Perhaps Augustine's most important contribution to our collective consciousness is to have carved an interior space deep within the soul; that familiar space known to us today as the self. By going through self-examination and inner struggle, Augustine deepens the hollows of the self and adds layers to what had previously only been conceived of as the general soul. The more Augustine withdrew, the deeper he burrowed into the region where the soul resides. At first, he found a place of inner turmoil. In the depths of this self, Augustine eventually found God as the source of his happiness and truth. Yet he labored intensely to get there.

Ironically, Augustine demonstrates to us how unhappiness may in fact point us to the source of our happiness: "I wish to bring back to mind my past foulness and the carnal corruptions of my soul. This is not because I love them, but that I may love you, my God. Out of love for your love I do this." It was in the absence of God, in the feeling of desire for Him and in his suffering without God, that Augustine found his happiness through God's love. "Over and over, I feel my wounds, not so much as inflicted upon me, but rather as healed by you."[77] In his distress, Augustine came to know of God retroactively, as He who healed his wounds.

Finding the transition to happiness may require a significant struggle. Augustine had to mend his divided will. He had to bear the weight of his love for God and silence the world and his carnal desires to refocus himself inwardly, where he could be supported by God. Augustine knew that happiness is found in the embrace of God's love, but he turned instead to sensual pleasures. He described himself as distended, reaching out to all sides from no center. His life had become "a living death."[78] But throughout all these trials, he never felt abandoned by

God. On the fateful day of his conversion, Augustine was de-spondent. He threw himself under a fig tree and wept. Then he heard the voice of a child, repeating the phrase "take up and read." Augustine interpreted this as the intervention of God's grace commanding him to open the Bible and read. He turned to St. Paul's Epistle to the Romans and was almost im-mediately converted. "Not in rioting and drunkenness, not in chambering and wantonness, not in strife and envying; but put ye on the Lord Jesus Christ, and make not provision for the flesh, in concupiscence. No further wished I to read, nor was there need to do so. Instantly, in truth, at the end of this sentence, as if before a peaceful light streaming into my heart, all dark shadows of doubt fled away."[79]

Augustine asks us to delve into our unhappiness and to see it as the way to our happiness. In his feeling of desire for com-pleteness and in his suffering, Augustine found happiness in the reciprocation of God's love. Yearning for our happiness, we too may have to wrangle with the depths of our desperation to find consistency in that which we love. Augustine was trans-formed by his love of God. No longer would he know himself in shame and error but in the glow of God's love. God served as the horizon through which he would come to know himself and the world. Loved by God, Augustine was free to become himself and to love others. He was free to embrace his best self, the self that he deemed to be in the image of God.

# APPLYING AUGUSTINE'S PHILOSOPHY

Augustine invites you to imagine your heart as a vast expanse full of gifts and clues to finding your happiness. Trust that you already know where your joy resides. Go inwardly and find the place in your soul that calls you to be calm. You have felt it before: look back to your memory. You already know what makes you happy, or you wouldn't know what to look for or how to recognize it once you have found it. For Augustine, God is the way to happiness. When he was far from God, his life felt insecure, hollow, and dispersed. When he loved God and was loved by God in return, he was calm and free from anxiety and fear. Explore the gaps between what brings you calm and joy, and what your habits push you to do. You may mistakenly be pursuing what brings you unhappiness.

Like the pull of gravity, your love is what carries and orients you. Be mindful of where you direct your love: differentiate the loves that leave you wanting from those that fill your soul. Remember, you are defined by what you love. Be careful not to give your love to just anyone or anything. Not all loves will nourish you. If you are unhappy, there may be a tension between your desire for immediate satisfaction and your long-term well-being, but more likely there is a tension between self-destructive behaviors and actions that are self-loving. Pay attention to inner conflicts and those moments when you are at war with yourself. Discord is a sign that you are in love with your own undoing. Use your unhappiness as a vehicle to arrive at your happiness. Allow your heart to guide you. When you are ready to claim your happiness, you will find your tolerance for damaging behaviors shrinking. Be ready for your beliefs and feelings to align, for your desires and actions to harmonize: prepare yourself for change. The truth of what you already know will surface to your consciousness when you are ready to hear it.

# QUESTIONS FOR CONSIDERATION

- *Are you pursuing what you love and are you fulfilled by it?*
- *Do you believe that you will be loved in return by who or what you give your love to?*
- *How do you understand Augustine's notion that your love is your weight by which you are carried?*
- *When are you at harmony with yourself and when are you at war with yourself?*
- *Can you identify self-destructive patterns in your life?*
- *What can you do to orient yourself toward self-love and away from self-harm?*
- *Are there any actions from your past that you regret, and what steps have you taken toward self-forgiveness?*
- *Are there any clues in your unhappiness that you may use to guide you to your happiness?*
- *What causes you to delay your happiness?*
- *Do you remember a time when you felt completely secure and free of anxiety?*
- *Are there any grounding forces in your life that provide you with a sense of calm?*

# Rumi

1207 AFGHANISTAN   1273 TURKEY

## *The Moon You Are Looking For Is Inside You*

Jalal-al-Din Mohamad Rumi is a philosopher of love. He asks us to take leave of caution and sober living to embrace the madness and oneness of divine love. A poet-philosopher, Rumi points to a place beyond thoughts and words, beyond fear and the boundaries and desires of the base self. This is the place of the heart, where renewal and transformation are possible. Rumi experienced this transformation through his love for the wandering Sufi mystic Shams of Tabriz: his teacher, friend, and likely lover. But it was with the loss of Shams and the metamorphosis of his grief into poetry that Rumi fully awoke to the ecstasy residing within him. "The result of my life is no more than three words: I was raw, I became cooked, I was burnt."[80] Devastated by his loss, then transformed through his pain, Rumi left his sober life as a Muslim cleric for the in-toxication of poetry, song, and dance. He asks us to welcome pain, loss, and anxiety as messengers bringing love, renewal, and transformation.

This being human is a guest house.
Every morning a new arrival.
A joy, a depression, a meanness,
some momentary awareness comes
as an unexpected visitor.
Welcome and entertain them all!
Even if they are a crowd of sorrows,
who violently sweep your house
empty of its furniture,
still, treat each guest honorably.
He may be clearing you out
for some new delight.
The dark thought, the shame, the malice.
meet them at the door laughing and invite them in.
Be grateful for whatever comes.
because each has been sent
as a guide from beyond.[81]

Rumi teaches us that pain can hold the key to an awakened heart. "These pains you feel are messengers—listen to them!"[82] Ordeals and hardships are there for our transformation. A mental breakdown could become a step toward emptying the self and carrying us to the other side, where we may receive life's bounty. Unlike philosophers who deny the senses in their pursuit of higher awareness, Rumi asks us to welcome them. The things we see, touch, smell, hear, and feel have the power to deliver us to a deeper understanding and appreciation of life; they are also where the unfolding of this appreciation takes place. "Sorrow prepares you for joy. It violently sweeps everything out of your house, so that new joy can find space to enter. It shakes the yellow leaves from the bough of your heart, so that fresh, green leaves can grow in their place."[83]

Rumi writes for those who have known despair and loss. He speaks to the mourners, the wanderers, and the despondent.

When we are broken, we become vulnerable. It is in this vulnerability that we lay our hearts open to the beauty of the world. Divinity is all around us. Wake up to the blessing that is life. Everything we need for our happiness lies within us, already complete. As Rumi writes, "The moon you are looking for is inside you."[84] He calls us to listen to the rhythms of our hearts and reminds us that those who do not hear the music think that the dancers are mad. There are many paths that lead to beauty and to the divine. Rumi chose the sensual path, founding the Sufi order of whirling dervishes. Dance and poetry were the vehicles he used to arrive at deep connection through love.

> Dance, when you're broken open. Dance, if you've torn the bandage off.
> Dance in the middle of the fighting. Dance in your blood.
> Dance, when you're perfectly free.
> Struck, the dancers hear a tambourine inside them,
> as a wave turns to foam on its very top, begin.
> Maybe you don't hear that tambourine, or the tree leaves clapping time.
> Close the ears on your head that listen mostly to lies and cynical jokes.
> There are other things to hear and see: dance-music and a brilliant city inside the Soul.
> Stretch your arms and take hold of the cloth of your clothes with both hands.
> The cure for pain is in the pain.
> Good and bad are mixed. If you don't have both, you don't belong with us.[85]

Pain is our messenger. It carries us through loss. The greatest loss is the loss of our egos or selves (*nafs* in Arabic). We see this loss of self in the rapture of Rumi's love for Shams. For three years, Rumi was absorbed with Shams. Suddenly, Shams disappeared. Rumi searched for him everywhere, but he was never to be seen again. Yet out of his suffering his union with Shams only grew. Shams' disappearance unraveled Rumi. But through his pain he underwent a transmutation of his base self into the pure self, as described in Sufi alchemy. Delving into the pain of his longing, Rumi came to understand that the love he was looking for was within him all along. "Goodbyes are only for those who love with their eyes."[86]

> I was dead, then alive.
> Weeping, then laughing.
> The power of love came into me,
> and I became fierce like a lion,
> then tender like the evening star.
> He said, "You're not mad enough.
> You don't belong in this house."
> I went wild and had to be tied up.
> He said, "Still not wild enough
> to stay with us!"
> I broke through another layer
> into joyfulness.
>
> He said, "It's not enough."
>
> I died.[87]

Rumi's poetry helps us remove the blockages from our hearts so that we can rise above the limitations of our ego selves. The *nafs* guards us against pain and shields us from the nakedness and vulnerability that is the condition of unconditional love. It prevents us from experiencing the depths of our emotions because it fears being carried away by something higher than itself. The heart demands risk and abandon, but the *nafs* turns from the unknown, ruled by the sobriety of reason. He asks us to empty ourselves of ego to receive love. "You who are not naked yet, you can go back to sleep."[88] Encumbered by the trappings and pull of our egos, we live always on the outside, seeking recognition everywhere but the inner chambers of our hearts. The ego seeks separation so that it may distinguish itself. Love seeks union. "When someone enters and says 'It is I,' I strike Him upon the head: 'This is the sanctuary of Love, you animal, Not a stable!'"[89]

Engaging in the heart-opening work of love requires practice, but above all it requires trust. Taking leave of the *nafs*, we awaken to the divinity within us and abandon ourselves to love and life—without fear, ego, or doubt. Complete surrender is Rumi's recipe for union with the divine.

> A lover doesn't figure the odds. He figures he came clean from God.
> As a gift without a reason, so he gives without cause or calculation or limit.
> A conventionally religious person behaves a certain way to achieve salvation.
> A lover gambles everything, the self, the circle around the zero!
> He or she cuts and throws it all away.
> This is beyond any religion.
> Lovers do not require from God any proof, or any text.
> Nor do they knock on a door to make sure this is the right street.
> They run, and they run.[90]

Rumi wants us to use our senses as a guide to the abundance of love and joy that lies within us: "The breeze at dawn has secrets to tell you. Don't go back to sleep. You must ask for what you really want. Don't go back to sleep."[91] He shows us how to use pain as a gateway to an open heart. When our hearts are open, we can join in union with something bigger than ourselves. Forgetting ourselves in the arms of the beloved, we join in the ecstatic union of love. To be infused and enveloped by the whole is the meaning of *tawid* (oneness in Arabic). *Tawid* describes a unity that is beyond high and low, me and you, here and there, and even beyond good and evil. Rumi writes of it thus: "My place is the Placeless, my trace is the Traceless; 'Tis neither body nor soul, for I belong to the soul of the Beloved. I have put duality away, I have seen that the two worlds are one; One I seek, One I know, One I see, One I call."[92]

When lovers unite, it is not as parts form a whole: rather their union forms the whole itself. "You are not a drop in the ocean. You are the entire ocean in a drop."[93] We must cease turning our sights outwardly in search of validation from the world or others. The alchemy of Sufism teaches us that everything we are looking for lies within us in abundance: "Don't look for it outside yourself. You are the source of milk. Don't milk others! There is a fountain inside you. Don't walk around with an empty bucket. You have a channel into the ocean, yet you ask for water from a little pool. Beg for the love expansion. Meditate only on THAT. The Qur'an says, And he is with you."[94]

Rumi teaches us to dance rather than to sleepwalk through life. There is nothing higher or more joyful than life. The world is our paradise, Rumi tells us: "You were born with wings, why prefer to crawl through life?"[95] Fasting from our thoughts, we must empty our selves of the *nafs* so that we may be filled with love: "Always be drunk, and come not toward Yourself—when you come toward yourself, you are Shackled."[96] Dying to our ego selves, we awaken to the place where the heart leads, unencumbered by the constraints of the world and mind. Rumi writes: "Inside this new love, die. Your way begins on the other side. Become the sky. Take an ax to the prison wall. Escape. Walk out like someone suddenly born into color. Do it now. You're covered with thick cloud. Slide out the side. Die, and be quiet. Quietness is the surest sign that you've died. Your old life was a frantic running from silence. The speechless full moon comes out now."[97]

It is never too late to fall in love. Hardened hearts may melt at any time. The door is always open. "Come, come, whoever you are," Rumi says. "Wanderer, worshipper, lover of living, it doesn't matter. Ours is not a caravan of despair. Come even if you have broken your vow a thousand times, Come, yet again, come, come."[98] For Rumi, love cannot be willed. We cannot rationalize our way to love or come to know the abandonment of love through the mind or the ego. We can only prepare ourselves for love through the vulnerability of an open heart. "Each night, the moon kisses secretly the lover who counts the stars."[99] Rumi had to travel the road of despair and suffer enormous pain over the loss of Shams before he came to rest in his heart. When we are broken, a crack appears through which we may be carried to the other side. Losing ourselves to the warmth of the sun, the sound of the ocean, or the touch of a loved one, we come to understand that we contain the universe within us.

To praise is to praise how one surrenders to the emptiness.
To praise the sun is to praise your own eyes.
Praise, the ocean. What we say, a little ship.
So the sea-journey goes on, and who knows where?
Just to be held by the ocean is the best luck
we could have. It's a total waking up!
Why should we grieve that we've been sleeping?
It doesn't matter how long we've been unconscious.
We're groggy, but let the guilt go.
Feel the motions of tenderness
around you, the buoyancy.[100]

# APPLYING RUMI'S PHILOSOPHY

When you feel most alone, Rumi is there. When you have lost the love of your life and are despondent, Rumi is there. Feel the warmth of the sun. Wake up to the joy that is your life. Throw off the shackles that bind your heart. All your feelings, happy or sad, are agents of life. Embrace your pain; don't run from it. Pain is your messenger—listen to it. Become vulnerable and open yourself to life's wonders. When you are broken you can begin to loosen the grip of your material self. Cast aside your ego and find yourself again in a unity with the universe. Delight in your senses and dance.

Rumi wants you to stop counting and calculating. Put your thoughts to rest and become a lover of existence rather than a thinker about existence. The world is your paradise. Use all your senses to experience your existence fully. Dying to your false self, you have the opportunity to be transformed. Embrace the mystery of life. Become lost in the arms of your beloved and be drunk in union with the divine. Like Rumi, spinning in the dance of a whirling dervish, allow all your pains and sorrows to spiral out into the universe. Dance and dance some more under the radiance of the moon and greet the world in its abundance. Become invigorated by the breeze and the light of the stars. Love with abandon and let down your defenses. When you have nothing to lose you have everything to gain. All you need already lies within you. Fill your emptiness and loss with love, laughter, and joy to walk the Sufi path laid out by Rumi.

# QUESTIONS FOR CONSIDERATION

- *Do you take time to appreciate the simple pleasures of nature, like the feel of a breeze or the sound of the ocean?*

- *Do you let yourself experience the pleasures that your senses bring, like the taste of a strawberry or the smell of a rose?*

- *Can you let go of your inhibitions and allow yourself to become intoxicated by the sheer beauty of existence?*

- *Can you identify any behaviors or thoughts that close your heart?*

- *Have you ever felt the boundaries of your ego dissolve into something greater?*

- *When do you let yourself be vulnerable?*

- *Do you allow yourself to dance with abandon and lose yourself in the music?*

- *Can you think about your pain as a messenger that may carry you to higher spiritual fulfillment?*

- *Have you ever been transformed by your pain?*

- *Have you ever thrown yourself into a person or a project with complete abandon, trusting that you are in the right place?*

- *Are you able to experience the love of someone you have lost by feeling them still around you?*

# René Descartes

1596 FRANCE   1650 SWEDEN

## Cogito Ergo Sum
## *I Think Therefore I Am*

René Descartes is a philosopher of reason. He is considered the father of modern Western philosophy because he located the foundations of all knowledge squarely in the power of rational thought. For Descartes, it is not enough to simply have beliefs; we must also be able to show why our beliefs are true through sound, rationally justified judgements. He asks us to guard against our prejudices and not to be too quick to judge based on insufficient knowledge or mere opinion. Doubt, confusion, and uncertainty all result from the misuse of our rational capacities and maintaining a blind faith in the truth of our senses. Not everything we see, feel, or hear is true: on the contrary, our senses often deceive us. Rational thinking, on the other hand, can isolate our emotions and cultural biases so that we can see things clearly and distinctly. Habits of the mind are difficult to break, but armed with a solid method and clear thinking, we arrive at truths that provide us with confidence. This is Descartes' message to us—by removing the impediments that cloud our thinking, we can relieve ourselves of doubt and see our way more clearly.

Descartes asks us to clean the houses of our minds. He wants us to take our preconceived ideas that we formed before developing our reason and put them under examination. This way, we will see if our truths are worthy of an independent rational agent. Before Descartes, what was deemed true varied according to custom, tradition, religion, or different schools of philosophical thought. After Descartes, for something to be true it had to be justified by the introspective powers of the reasoning mind. Yet, Descartes had to tread lightly when touting reason as the vehicle for arriving at truth. Church authorities ruthlessly condemned anyone standing against its main tenets. The highest of these tenets was that only God had access to the truth. Descartes witnessed the Roman Catholic Church's attacks against Galileo: Descartes, like Galileo, supported Copernicus' findings that the earth moves around the sun. Judiciously, Descartes courted the Church's approval by dedicating his work to the Church. His ideas would cast a devastating blow to its authority, however, by giving individuals the power to independently secure truths for themselves through the exercise of their reason. "I shall bring to light the true riches of our souls," Descartes writes, "opening up to each of us the means whereby we confined within ourselves without any help from anyone else all the knowledge that we may need for the conduct of life."[101]

Descartes' project was to secure a firm foundation for the sciences. He wanted to arrive at universal truths through the reasoning powers of the subject, rather than through divine revelation or outside authorities. He likens this search to tearing down the walls of a house built upon weak foundations so as to rebuild it on more solid ones. As with his discoveries in the fields of optics, physics, and mathematics, he had hoped to secure as solid a foundation for all sciences and philosophy. Writing amidst wide skepticism about the ability of science to know anything with certainty, Descartes' search for truth begins, ironically, by employing the very methods of skepticism against itself. He introduces what has come to be known as the method of doubt: he vows to reject any thought as true that is subject to even the slightest doubt. Descartes sets out to find just one principle that is true and beyond all doubt. Upon this principle, he would be able to build further knowledge. If his search were to prove unsuccessful, he would concede along with the skeptics that true knowledge is impossible. "Archimedes sought but one firm and immovable point in order to move the entire earth from one place to another. Just so, great things are also to be hoped for if I succeed in finding just one thing, however slight, that is certain and unshaken."[102]

Descartes empowers us to arrive at our own conclusions by asking us to follow a solid method that guides us to think more rationally. He believes that we are all equipped with reason, but not all of us lead our minds in the right direction: "For it is not enough to have a good mind; the main thing is to apply it well."[103] The ideas in our minds have a great bearing on our actions and therefore should be subject to rational justification. Our opinions and ideas may indeed be based on faulty foundations that cannot pass the test of reason. When we feel confused or our ideas are cloudy, it is likely that there are inconsistencies in our thinking. To ensure that our thoughts are not being led astray by habits of anxiety or muddied by emotions, Descartes asks us to delve into our minds and rationally meditate about the strength of our convictions. By directing our minds properly, we will arrive at sound, rationally justified judgments.

Turning inwardly to the resources of his own mind, Descartes vows to trust no authority other than his own in his search for truth: "I would not have believed I ought to rest content for a single moment with the opinion of others, had I not proposed to use my own judgement to examine them when there was time."[104] Since we generally think that what we see, hear, and touch is true, Descartes asks us to begin by employing his method of doubt to question the validity of knowledge gained through our senses. He wonders if he could be mistaken about whether he is sitting in a gown by the fire. He remembers how he sometimes erroneously thinks that images in his dreams are real, or that he is awake when he is in fact asleep. "How often, asleep at night, am I convinced of just such familiar events—that I am here in my dressing-gown, sitting by the fire–when in fact I am lying undressed in bed!"[105] He also recalls how objects he sees in water appear bent when they are really straight, and how the sun appears to us as small when it is in fact many times larger.

Staying true to his method, Descartes does not have to prove that something is definitely false to question its truth. He only needs to show that it is open to doubt. From the above examples, Descartes is forced to concede that nothing our senses show us can be deemed beyond doubt as the senses have been known to deceive us. And since we know our bodies through our senses, Descartes even wonders whether he actually exists or whether he could be living in a dream. But then he asks "Is it not I who am doing this doubting? Am I not the one questioning whether I exist?" He concludes that no amount of doubting can bring him to doubt his own existence. This is because he, Descartes, is doing the doubting and therefore must exist. However, he is doubting not as a body but as a thinking, rational being: "I am, I exist—that is certain."[106] Descartes has finally found something that is true beyond doubt. As long as he thinks, he exists as a thinking mind. This is the thought behind his famous statement, *cogito ergo sum*: "I think, therefore I am."[107]

By asserting the "I" or the rational thinking mind as his first principle of philosophy, Descartes shows us how we may overcome doubt through reflection upon our own thinking. Significantly, however, at this juncture Descartes is certain only that he is a thinking mind with ideas. He has yet to prove the existence of his body, which, like other material bodies, he has shown may not be real. For Descartes the mind and the body are made of two different substances. He has to backtrack later in his argument to show that his body is real and to explain how two different substances relate to each other. Ultimately, he concludes that his mind is to his body as a sailor is to a ship. Indeed the mind and body are closely intermingled. Despite Descartes' mind-body dualism, he secures a foundation for science by showing that justification is sought internally. It is found in the mind turning back on itself and adhering to strict standards of thought. Through the experiential relation we have with our minds in rational reflection, we can become the foundation of our own knowledge.

Descartes teaches that when we direct our minds to perceive something "clearly and distinctly," we can be confident that what we perceive is true: ". . . if, whenever I have to make a judgment, I restrain my will so that it extends to what the intellect clearly and distinctly reveals, and no further, then it is quite impossible for me to go wrong."[108] Ideas that are clearly present to our minds—an observed image, a twinge of pain—are real. However, for them to be true they must also be distinct and transparent so as not to be confused with anything else. If it is possible that a pain felt in the eye actually originates in the head, or that a feeling of distrust toward a person arises from one's own propensity toward suspicion, then the idea is not distinct. It should not be acted upon as if it were true. Our pains and pleasures may guide us in the discovery of what we hold to be true, but they should not be taken as true at face value without being put to the test of reason. Feelings are not facts.

Descartes asks us to listen to our minds rather than to our hearts or to our senses. To hammer home the point that it is reason and not our senses that provides us with solid truths, Descartes introduces the example of a piece of wax. What happens if we take a piece of wax from the honeycomb and place it next to the fire? It melts, and is no longer identifiable to our senses as the same piece of wax. Nevertheless, Descartes contends, we know that it *is* the same piece of wax. But our senses do not discover this truth, since the wax is no longer recognizable to any of our senses. It has changed in shape, texture, and size. Rather, it is reason, Descartes' *cogito*, that grasps the true nature of the wax. Through the powers of reason, we are able to recognize the melted wax as the same piece of wax despite the changes in its appearance.

When we feel conflicted and in doubt, we would be wise to follow Descartes' advice and use reason to arrive at clarity through logic and introspection. By breaking down large problems into their more basic components, clarifying our definitions, and abstracting our emotions from our thinking, we may attain confidence in our thoughts. We can gain stability and resolution in our actions. What is true and good for us gives us pleasure, specifically the pleasure of equanimity that is free from doubt. But perhaps Descartes could have better followed his findings and attended to the clear and distinct signs of his own body. He accepted an invitation by Queen Christina of Sweden to study at her court and give her lessons in philosophy. A nocturnal creature by nature and plagued by weak health, Descartes nevertheless accommodated the Queen's request to begin lessons at 5:00A.M. Unused to the extreme cold and harsh Swedish winter, and certainly not accustomed to waking so early, Descartes caught a respiratory infection. Within months of his stay in Sweden, he was dead. In despair, the Queen converted to Catholicism and shortly gave up her throne to become a traveling philosopher, perhaps following in the footsteps of her most admired thinker.

*Philosophy Wise*

# APPLYING DESCARTES' PHILOSOPHY

Descartes asks you to meditate on the strength of your truths by putting them to the test of reason. He shows you how to overcome doubt by retreating into your own mind. By doing this you can take stock of your thoughts and emotions and submit them to the power of rational thought. Impediments to clear thinking consist in unfounded opinions, beliefs, biases, and ideas that make it difficult to separate truth from error. Anxieties, fears about the future, emotions, prejudices, and habits of thought also block the way to clear thinking. If you are conflicted or in doubt, it is likely that your ideas are not clear or distinctly separated from other ideas that are clouding your thinking. Search for signs of anxiety and inconsistency in your thoughts. These are clues that your mind is leading you astray: your thinking may be muddled by emotions, desires, or personal biases.

Approach your problems and questions by breaking them down to their most basic components. It is easier to see a problem clearly and distinctly when you have gotten to its core elements. Trust in your own authority to arrive at the truth and communicate with more precision. Speak concisely about the matter at hand and make sure your words aren't charged with emotion, to better get your point across without hurting others' feelings. Your ideas are all up for dispute; you should be able to change your mind by arriving at clarity through rational assessment. Take the time to reflect on your reasoning about the world and your feelings. Your pains and pleasures are guides to help you discover what you deem to be true, but be careful not to judge everything you see or feel as truth. Act with conviction and overcome doubt by trusting your capacity to apply a rational standard to your beliefs. When you are too quick to judge, you are liable to act on false knowledge or mere opinion. Clarity in your thinking will help you arrive at sound judgments that can be rationally justified so that you may act and communicate with confidence.

# QUESTIONS FOR CONSIDERATION

– *Can you rationally support the principles and ideas that you hold to be true and beyond doubt?*

– *Do you think it is important to justify your beliefs?*

– *Are you able to clearly explain the rationale for your actions?*

– *What criteria do you use to judge what is true and what is false?*

– *Do you need to examine any long-held beliefs that you have taken for granted?*

– *Do you guard against unexamined opinions, anxieties, or prejudices that may cloud your vision or distort your judgment?*

– *Do your emotions, habits, or prejudices encroach on your thinking about serious matters?*

– *How would your life benefit if you clarified your thoughts and removed the emotions and insecurities that cloud your thinking?*

– *Are there times when you have hurt others by reacting emotionally?*

– *Is there anything that you hold to be true and beyond doubt? If so, how does it shape how you see the world and relate to others?*

# Immanuel Kant

1724 PRUSSIA   1804 PRUSSIA

## *Live as Though Your Every Act Were to Become a Universal Law*

Kant is a philosopher of integrity. He teaches us that integrity is rooted in acting consistently according to rational moral principles that are transparent for everyone else to follow. Each of us is endowed with the power to reason and to establish laws for ourselves that we regularly obey. These laws are our principles. Before Kant, matters of right and wrong were generally decided by religious, legal, or cultural authorities, which varied according to time and place. The force of these dictates was often tied to reward and punishment. Kant asks us not to act morally out of self-interest. We should not act out of a desire for a reward, like going to heaven, or because we fear punishment by legal authorities. For Kant, we are moral only if we act according to rational laws that are applicable to all rational agents.

Our worth is internal to us. It lies in the capacity to abide by our principles and stick to them regardless of what we have to win by acting against them, or how others treat us. Kant is keenly aware that our thoughts and actions are influenced by personal gain, cultural prejudices, and emotions, which can change daily. This is why he introduces reason as the steward for moral action. Each of us is endowed with the power to reason and to establish laws for ourselves that we regularly obey. By sticking to rational principles, we remain stable despite our changing circumstances.

For Kant, we are moral only if we act consistently out of duty. If we rely on our moods, or the outside world for our motivations to act, then we will be tossed around with the changing tides. Others will be unable to depend on us, and we ourselves will lack substance. Rising above personal inclinations, self-interest, and external motivations, is how we act with integrity by following principles that others may follow by thinking rationally and without contradiction. To be consistent and unified in action and thought, to be at one with ourselves by adhering to our principles, is to have integrity and to realize our humanity to the fullest. Integrity is the backbone of what it means to be a consistent moral self throughout changing situations. Acting on the basis of principles that we follow regardless of circumstances, we gain the confidence of stability and the trust of others.

Kant asks us not to treat some people better than others by virtue of their wealth, power, popularity, or what they can do for us. To be a moral agent means treating others with dignity, just as we would wish them to act toward us. This is his principle of humanity, whereby we accord absolute respect to ourselves and to others by virtue of our shared capacity to reason. Reason is the highest human power; through reason we are both the legislature and subject of our own laws. Reason is the faculty that allows us to rise above the vagaries of religious, cultural, and personal beliefs to set laws for ourselves.

While some entrust religious authorities with securing our moral principles, Kant puts his faith in the autonomy of individuals and our ability to reason. He helped usher in the age of European Enlightenment by asking us to think for ourselves instead of blindly following in obedience to external authorities: "*Sapere Aude*! Have the courage to use your own understanding!—that is the motto of enlightenment."[109] Allowing others to think for us is what Kant calls a self-imposed immaturity. Immaturity is characterized by the lack of courage to use our own reasoning powers to break free from external supports or guidance. "It is so easy to be immature. If I have a book to serve as my understanding, a pastor to serve as my conscience, a physician to determine my diet for me, and so on, I need not exert myself at all. I need not think if only I can pay: others will readily undertake the irksome work for me."[110] Rules, formulas, and other substitutes for independent thinking are "the shackles of a permanent immaturity."[111] Instead, Kant asks us to become mature through the exercise of independent thought.

Kant asks what it means to be good, and sets out to establish a universal moral theory built on rationality alone. Reason is the faculty that allows us to lay down laws in the form of duties, and to act out of duty. To help us to act consistently and with integrity despite our personal inclinations, prejudices, or beliefs, Kant introduces a formula for moral action called the Categorical Imperative: "Act in such a way as to treat humanity, whether in your own person or in that of anyone else, always as an end and never merely as a means."[112] This means we should act toward others in ways that promote their autonomy. We must be careful not to treat people merely as a means: as vehicles for gaining something we want.

Kant provides numerous examples of what it means to act consistently according to his Categorical Imperative. If a shopkeeper returns change to a customer who has overpaid only in the hope of getting a good reputation and building up her business, she is not acting morally. She is acting rather with an eye toward personal gain. Such an action is neither moral nor dignified because it treats the customer as a means toward the shopkeeper's ends. But acting according to self-interest also compromises our own integrity, because our outward actions do not match our inward intentions. For Kant, morality is not subject to economic exchanges of reward or punishment. Rather, morality is worthy in itself. It is worthy as that by which we accord absolute respect to ourselves and to each other by virtue of our shared humanity and capacity to reason.

This is what it means to be a moral agent for Kant: to treat others with respect as would we have them treat us, "not from external motive or future advantage, but rather from the idea of the dignity of a rational being who obeys no law except that which he himself gives while obeying it."[113] In Kant's moral theory, what matters are our motives and intentions, not the consequences of our actions.

Another formulation of the Categorical Imperative reads: "Act as if the maxim of your action were to become through your will a universal law of nature."[114] By this, Kant means that we should establish a law for ourselves that we could will to be a law for all humanity. If I say, for example, that it is acceptable for me to lie and borrow money with the intention of not paying it back, then I must agree that all people have this same right. But when we apply the Categorical Imperative to this issue, we see that lying involves a contradiction of reason. If we posit as a universal law that lying is permissible to get out of a difficult situation, then we state as a maxim that for all people lying is permissible under distress. However, if this principle were a universal law, then the entire concept of promising would lose its meaning: no one would loan anyone money because we could not trust that it would be paid back. For us to successfully borrow money, we need the concept of a promise to exist and to be valid. The law is therefore inconsistent and cannot be a principle that is binding for all rational agents.

Kant believes lying is wrong not because of any religious law or cultural standard, but because it is logically inconsistent. When we use reason to guide our moral actions, we must agree that the same rules apply to all people. If we cannot universalize a maxim, then it is immoral to act upon it. To universalize a maxim means to act upon it as though it were binding for all human beings at all times.

However, lying also fails the test of the Categorical Imperative, because when we lie to others we rob them of the ability to reason and judge for themselves. We treat them as a means to our selfish ends rather than as rational agents. When we lie to someone and present them with false information, we make it impossible for them to make an informed and responsible decision based on true information. We rob not only the other person of their integrity but also ourselves. This is because we are one person when we lie and another person who knows the truth behind the lie. For Kant, conflict and contradiction speak of a divided will: a self that is not whole and lacks integrity.

Kant so valued consistency that it was said that his neighbors in Königsberg would set their watches by the punctuality of his walks. But it was in the realm of morality that Kant thinks humanity's highest value is found. He deems human life priceless, valuable in itself by virtue of our shared ability to act according to rationally chosen principles. Abiding by our principles regardless of circumstance or desire, we become masters over ourselves. Kant considers such mastery the crown of human achievement. "Two things fill the mind with ever new and increasing admiration and awe, the more often and steadily we reflect upon them: the starry heavens above me and the moral law within me."[115]

# APPLYING KANT'S PHILOSOPHY

Kant wants you to know that you are special, but what makes you special is what makes other people special as well—the power to create and live by principles that are universally applicable to all rational beings. For Kant, your greatest good is your integrity and humanity. Only humans can think and choose to act against their impulses, inclinations, and desires to abide by self-created moral principles. When you act on principle despite how others treat you and despite personal gain, you act with integrity on the basis of duty. Become a law unto yourself. Don't let your actions be guided by your emotions, prejudices, and most of all your self-interest; rather let them be guided by principles. Your worth is internal to you and lies in your capacity to lay down laws for yourself that you consistently follow despite changes in your circumstances.

Stand firmly on the ground of rational principles and find your power as a moral and rational agent. When you live by principles that you deem worthy for all others to follow, then your actions will be transparent to others. Win the respect and trust of others by treating everyone equally and with dignity. How you treat others says everything about who you are and how you expect to be treated. Don't sell your integrity for material gain or to win a popularity contest. Integrity is your superpower. Sometimes only you will know how principled your actions are. Making consistent ethical choices, you gain the confidence of stability and the admiration of others who can depend on you to act out of duty, and not on the basis of how you may be feeling on any given day.

# QUESTIONS FOR CONSIDERATION

- *Do you act from your principles, or do you allow self-interest to determine your actions?*

- *Are the principles that guide your life transparent for others to see?*

- *Can you turn the principles that you live by into universal laws for others to follow?*

- *Do you inspire confidence and trust in others by acting out of duty and principle?*

- *Are you consistent in your behavior, or do you act a certain way one day and a different way the next day according to your desires?*

- *Do you provide others with the conditions for exercising their freedom and living lives of integrity?*

- *Do you acknowledge other people's capacity to think autonomously for themselves by being truthful to them so they can make informed choices?*

- *Do you take the time to get the right information so that you may make reasoned decisions?*

- *Do you betray your integrity by acting in ways that please others?*

- *Do you think all people are equally worthy of respect, or do you treat some people with more respect than others?*

- *Do you treat others as you want them to treat you?*

# Søren Kierkegaard

1813 DENMARK   1855 DENMARK

## *The Most Common Form of Despair Is Not Being Who You Are*

Søren Kierkegaard is a philosopher of a leap of faith. He believes that each of us has a unique truth that belongs to us alone. This is our subjective truth. It can only be found by going inwardly to discover our passion. Reason and calculating thought are powerless before passion. This is because there are no objective measures to weigh the value of a subjective truth. Rational calculations cannot help us find our passion, or guarantee that following it will lead us to happiness. A risk is always involved when choosing a way of life that has its certainty only in the self. This is why a leap of faith is required to act on a truth that is gauged by the passion with which we live our lives. Kierkegaard describes subjective truth as follows: "Here is such a definition of truth: An objective uncertainty, held fast through appropriation with the most passionate inwardness, is the truth, the highest truth available for an existing person.

At the point where the road swings off (and where that is cannot be stated objectively, since it is precisely subjectivity), objective knowledge is suspended. Objectively he then has only uncertainty, but this is precisely what intensifies the infinite passion of inwardness, and truth is precisely the daring venture of choosing the objective uncertainty with the passion of the infinite."[116]

We meet Kierkegaard at the precipice of life defining choices. Standing at the fork of a significant decision whose outcome is uncertain provokes anxiety. But existence cannot be rid of contradictions, or of the anxiety of having to choose between different ways of life with no guarantee of success. Either this, or that, but not both. Something is always lost in making a choice. When we pursue one way of life, we must close the door to other possible pathways available to us. Making a commitment to live our truth, we encounter a "crisis of faith," as we must let the possibilities we have not chosen pass us by. However, to not choose a self—a truth—for fear of closing off the other options before us, is to fail to set down roots and build a history for ourselves. For Kierkegaard, this is the mark of despair: "The most common form of despair is not being who you are."[117]

Rejecting the more traditional academic pursuit of attaining knowledge and certainty of the outside world through rational truths, Kierkegaard turns inward to explore the uncertainty of individuals' concrete lived existence. This is a way of philosophizing that has come to be called existentialism. For Kierkegaard, everyday existence is too complex and individual to be reduced to the generalities of abstract truths. Rather, his philosophy of existence asks us to go within ourselves to listen to the voice of our own personal and passionate truth: a truth that we would be willing to live and die for. It may be difficult to hear this voice through the noise of a lifetime of conditioning and outside pressures to conform to a more secure and packaged way of life. It is certainly difficult to act on an inner truth whose certainty is measured by a passion that has no rational basis, and that cannot be validated by any outside authority. This is why a leap of faith is required.

To characterize the road from despair to faith, Kierkegaard depicts three stages of life: the aesthetic, the ethical, and the religious. As a thinker of choice and individuality, he cannot preach any specific directives on how to live an authentic life. This is why he uses indirect communication and pseudonyms to present the reader with a variety of choices from the different perspectives of those who live the life they describe. For Kierkegaard, the aesthetic individual represents despair because they fail to commit to a way of life but rather thrive off "the sweet pastry of possibility."[118] Nothing anchors or holds down the aesthete's choices; every decision or way of life may easily be overturned or replaced by another, "having been built upon that which can both be and not be."[119] Consequently, the aesthetic individual fails to commit to a subjective truth or to any one way of life. They therefore fail to build a history. Kierkegaard's ethical individual turns to the aesthetic and asks: "Is it not painful to let life go by in this way without ever finding solidarity in it; is it not sad, my young friend, that life never acquires content for you?"[120]

Against the fragmentation and rootlessness of aesthetic existence, Kierkegaard's ethical individual shows an understanding of the gravity of life. The ethical individual chooses to find fulfillment in committing to universal principles that are consistent and socially recognized. Marriage is the prime example by which the ethical individual builds a history and gives content to their life through a lifetime of shared memories and practices.

But the highest stage for Kierkegaard is the religious way of life, although he was a staunch opponent of organized religion.

He challenged the Church's claim to truth through its proximity to divine revelation. For Kierkegaard, truth does not come from above, but from within. It comes to us through a passionate relationship to existence realized in the mundane practices of our everyday lives. In the religious way of life that Kierkegaard upholds there are no universal principles of right and wrong. There are no objective truths that may guide us or provide us with certainty, as there are for the ethical individual. A leap of faith is required. The biblical character Abraham illustrates this leap of faith. He is Kierkegaard's paradigmatic figure of the religious individual.

As the story goes, Abraham and Sarah are unable to conceive a child. In their old age, God blesses them with a boy they name Isaac. Then the unspeakable happens. God asks Abraham to sacrifice his son. Kierkegaard is rendered sleepless contemplating the anxiety of Abraham's "trial of faith" and wonders whether readers of this story truly understand the magnitude of Abraham's decision. Perhaps we think that Abraham simply follows in an act of compliance with God's command. But Kierkegaard draws out the anxiety that must have attended Abraham's decision to sacrifice his only son. He wonders: how could Abraham be certain that it was God speaking to him, rather than Satan, or the delusions of a feeble, aging mind? How could Abraham be sure that he was not dreaming when he thought he heard God speak to him? What kind of God would demand such a sacrifice?

Kierkegaard suggests that Abraham has every motivation to seek alternative interpretations for what was being asked of him. From the perspective of the ethical individual, Abraham would be considered a murderer. If he were to share his crisis with anyone, his sanity would be questioned. His wife Sarah would surely act swiftly to protect her son. Who could help Abraham in the choice confronting him? Here, Kierkegaard explains, Abraham stands alone with his passion and his faith. With fear and trembling, Abraham takes a leap of faith and proceeds up the mountain to sacrifice his son. In doing so, he chooses himself as the father of faith. Ultimately, Abraham wins Isaac back and a lamb is sacrificed in his place.

Each of us has our own truth. Just like Abraham we must stand alone in the face of uncertainty to choose ourselves as single individuals through the passion of our inwardness. Indeed, Kierkegaard states, eventually we come to realize that the most important truths are beyond understanding. They unfold when we allow ourselves to be overcome by our passion and truth. Most think, he writes, "that life is simply a matter of understanding more and more, and that if it were granted to them to live longer, that life would continue to be one long continuous growth in understanding. How many of them ever experience the maturity of discovering that there comes a critical moment where everything is reversed, after which the point becomes to understand more and more that there is something which cannot be understood."[121] For Kierkegaard, it is one thing to live poetically and quite another to have our lives be poetically composed by our passions.

Ironically, Kierkegaard claims to have been unable to make a leap of faith: "I cannot make the movement of faith. I cannot shut my eyes and plunge confidently into the absurd; it is for me an impossibility, but I do not praise myself for that."[122] Yet he seems to have made such a leap when he ended his engagement to Regina, his one and only love, although he would characterize this choice as a necessity. Kierkegaard thought himself plagued by his family's curse of depression and therefore unfit to live the repetition of everyday life required by marriage. He claims to stand in awe of those "knights of faith" who are able to live their passion and realize the sublime and infinite in their mundane existence. He contrasts the knight of faith to the "knight of infinite resignation," who holds fast to the impossible—to his love for a princess, for example—but who is unable to live the impossible when it becomes a reality. When the absurd happens and the princess reciprocates the knight's love, he turns away from realizing love in the real world. He prefers to hold onto the eternal love he has for her in his imagination.

In Kierkegaard's brand of Christian existentialism, we commit ourselves completely by virtue of faith to an idea, a life, a love, or in Kierkegaard's case God. Concentrating our passion into a leap, we decide to commit to our truth and live the sublime, the uncertain certainty of our passion, in our everyday pedestrian lives. By saying "no" to the obligations of marriage, Kierkegaard took a leap of faith to choose himself as the thinker of individual subjective truth. His concepts of freedom, decision, despair, anxiety, authenticity, finitude, passionate existence, and subjective truth have come to define the philosophy of existentialism that was made popular by the atheists Jean-Paul Sartre and Simone de Beauvoir. Kierkegaard asks us to move from a leap to a walk by giving content to our passions through our everyday historical existence. By landing on our feet after a leap, we engage passionately in the simple acts of our everyday lives to secure for ourselves an authentic existence.

# APPLYING KIERKEGAARD'S
# PHILOSOPHY

Kierkegaard asks you to go inwardly into yourself and find your passion. There is a truth that belongs to you alone—a subjective certainty that lies deeply embedded within you. But this truth cannot be found by reason or through rational calculations. Subjective truth is objectively uncertain. Your truth is a matter of choice, gauged by passion, validated by faith, and executed in a leap. Let your passion be the measure of your truth. You may choose to live by taking the safe route, the one that you reason will bring you the most benefit or security, or you can take a leap of faith to follow your passion. But there is no guarantee of success. Objective certainty is what scientists and mathematicians use to measure their truths: existence, however, is uncertain. It therefore requires a leap in the face of anxiety.

Risk your security and choose your truth. Let go of calculating thought and be prepared to confront the anxiety that signals and accompanies a leap of faith. There is always a risk involved before the radical choice of your truth. Certainty enters only when the existential crisis of choosing a unique and authentic way of life is averted. Take actions that reflect the life that is most true to you. To live without commitments, always in the midst of pure possibility, is to be detached from your life. Detachment destroys historical existence and leaves you with a fragmented and rootless self, always willing to give up one path for another. Suspended before a decision to choose your truth you will likely face a crisis of faith. Make a choice and stand firmly in the truth of your subjectivity to secure a passionate relationship to your life. Transform your anxiety and uncertainty into the truth of your existence. This is how you build a history for yourself by committing to the person you have chosen to be. The history you create is the hallmark of authenticity.

# QUESTIONS FOR CONSIDERATION

- *Do you relate to your life personally and passionately?*

- *Do you allow your passion to overwhelm you and bring you to your subjective truth, or do you make your decisions based on rational deliberation?*

- *Are you fleeing from any decisions that require a leap of faith because of the risk of uncertainty?*

- *Are you afraid to limit your choices by committing to a way of life, wishing instead to remain open to all possibilities?*

- *Are you leaving things ambiguous in your life because you fear making choices and commitments?*

- *Can you confront the anxiety you feel before an important life decision and take a leap of faith?*

- *Are you able to take a leap, and risk a certain now for a future "maybe"?*

- *Have you chosen the life you are living or are you following along with what life has thrown your way?*

- *Are you committed to the life you have chosen and the person you have chosen to be?*

- *Does your life have meaning, supported by commitments that allow you to develop a history?*

- *Are you able to view the events in your life as part of a personal narrative, with a beginning, middle, and future end?*

# Friedrich Nietzsche

1844 GERMANY   1900 GERMANY

## Was That Life?
## *Well, Then! Once More!*

Nietzsche is a philosopher of self-creation. He asks us to be better versions of ourselves by following our instincts, to become who we are without apology—to become the *Übermensch* (overman). A self-proclaimed psychologist of the soul who provocatively refers to himself in his book *Ecce Homo* as the "Antichrist," Nietzsche inspires us to philosophize with a hammer. He asks us to throw away all inhibitions and moral guides and embark on a path of our own self-creation. Trusting in the forces of our instinct and will, he calls upon us to take leave of faith and the desire for certainty and instead to dance near the abyss. What is most ours is what makes us feel beautiful and strong. What does not belong to us is what weakens and drains us of our power. For Nietzsche, what does not kill us makes us stronger. "He enjoys only what is good for him; his pleasure, his desire, ceases when the limits of what is good for him are overstepped. He divines remedies against injuries; he knows how to turn serious accidents to his own advantage; whatever does not kill him makes him stronger."[123]

Nietzsche asks us to affirm life with a "triumphant yes-saying to oneself."[124] The highest value of life is life itself—not just any life, but a happy life that is worth repeating. It is a form of sickness to try to rationalize our instincts or our lives. For Nietzsche, that which needs to be proved is not worth much. He wants us to heal ourselves from self-doubt and all forms of crippling self-consciousness to live as "free spirits." Creating values that enhance our strength and power, we live confidently and in openness with ourselves through a joyful existence. Affirming the life we have now, in good times and bad, and wishing for nothing to be different, is Nietzsche's formula for greatness. This affirmation is called *amor fati*, or the love of one's fate: "The ideal of the most high-spirited, alive, and world-affirming human being who has not only come to terms and learned to get along with whatever was and is, but who wants to have what was and is repeated into all eternity, shouting insatiably *da capo*—[.]"[125] "Was *that* life? Well then! Once more!"[126]

Nietzsche interprets the history of philosophy in a uniquely physiological way, seeing it as guided by either healthy or diseased instincts. While science promotes the idea of objective truth, Nietzsche thinks that all truths and values are matters of perception and interpretation. They provide us with the necessary fictions we need to live. Truth is a creation, a process of doing. For Nietzsche, truths and values arise from either healthy instincts, which are life affirming and enhance power, or unhealthy instincts that promote weakness and negate life. As a champion of instinct, Nietzsche makes an enemy of reason. He argues that reason was born out of a fear of the unknown and the need to alleviate this fear by imposing logic upon the world and making the unfamiliar familiar: "With the unknown, one is confronted with danger, discomfort... the first instinct is to abolish these painful states... First principle: any explanation is better than none." Nietzsche credits Socrates with introducing the use of reason out of his own fear of the irrational.

The result is a world stripped of its mystery: "The harshest daylight, rationality at any cost, life bright, cold, circumspect, conscious, without instinct, in opposition to the instincts, has itself become no more than a form of sickness."[127]

However, the greatest affront to instinct, he believes, is the Judeo–Christian tradition, which has lost touch with life-affirming instincts. In Nietzsche's eyes, the dawn of Christianity brought a sense of empowerment to the naturally weak of spirit. It replaced a very different world where noble aristocrats lived by strong and healthy instincts. What made these nobles feel strong, they called good; what weakened them, they called bad. Nietzsche argues that with the rise of Judeo-Christian morality, values were born in reaction; they were born out of resentment toward the nobles and their strength-promoting values. Christian morality revolts against life-affirming instincts by giving rise to a "slave morality," which gains its strength in numbers. It is therefore also dubbed a "herd morality."

Nietzsche thinks there is no creative deed in slave morality. Slave morality consists in saying "no" to life: its action is from the ground up a reaction. What slave morality considers bad is everything valued as good by the aristocrats: strength, power, war, and instinct. Everything that is deemed bad by the nobles is revalued by slave morality as good. The slaves would thus declare that "the miserable alone are the good; the poor, powerless, lowly alone are the good."[128] For Nietzsche, suffering and waiting for a better world to come are signs of no longer knowing how to seek our advantages or declare our wants and needs. Nietzsche calls this "nihilism": the period when our drives and instincts work against us. "To have to combat one's instincts—that is the formula for decadence: as long as life is ascending, happiness and instinct are one."[129] This is the story Nietzsche tells of how the human animal and society become sick by turning against instinct, power, and strength.

Against the no-saying of Christian morality, Nietzsche says "yes" to life. Indeed, he proclaims that God is dead and that we moderns have unwittingly killed Him with our devotion to science, individualism and ambition and our lack of faith and piety. With the death of a creator and universal truths, we no longer have a guarantee for the sanctity of certain values and pre-ordained truths. With no universal foundation for establishing the meaning of life, Nietzsche asks us rather to become artists of our lives and create values that support our power. Values do not come from above but from below. They are rooted in healthy instincts: "You look up when you feel the need for elevation. And I look down because I am elevated."[130] Standing in our power, we learn to forget easily, to have enemies, and even to respect our opponents. Nietzsche admires Greek tragedy because it testifies to a spirit that gives form and definition to the ecstatic energy of life through the creation of art, without robbing it of its dynamism and raw instinct. This wisdom of affirming life through art provides the model for Nietzsche's idea of a "grand style."

Nietzsche asks us to become who we are and live as free spirits without regret. We do this through self-creation in beauty. Freedom and joy manifest outwardly in a grand existence. The strong have an instinct for what makes them stronger, more powerful, and more vibrant: "a well-constituted human being, a 'happy one,' must perform certain actions and instinctively shrinks from other actions."[131] We live in a grand style by giving form to our instincts, thus creating our lives as works of art. In tune with our natural strengths, with what enhances rather than diminishes our power, we create beauty even out of our weaknesses and flaws. But unlike natural instincts that require no work, beauty and power must be created. Surveying our strengths and weaknesses, Nietzsche asks us to transform what we dislike about ourselves into an artistic plan that delights the eye. [132] He writes that "Every artist knows how far from any feeling of letting himself go his 'most natural' state is."[133]

In a grand style, we artfully fit our instincts into a unique way of life that is attuned to what makes us feel strong, powerful, and healthy. Organizing our many disparate parts into a coherent and harmonious style requires discipline and self-awareness. What matters is not whether our tastes are good or bad, but that we each have a single taste. Bringing our essential characteristics into harmony with our instincts to promote our strength and health is Nietzsche's formula for a beautiful life. This is how we live in a grand style, and affirm what most belongs to us. "The highest feeling of power and security finds expression in that which possesses grand style. Power which no longer requires proving; which disdains to please; which is slow to answer; which is conscious of no witness around it; which lives oblivious of the existence of any opposition; which reposes in itself, fatalistic, a law among laws: that is what speaks of itself in the form of grand style."[134]

To test the health of our instincts and how highly we value our lives, Nietzsche suggests a thought experiment that he calls the "eternal recurrence of the same," or the "eternal return." This thought experiment asks us to stop and consider whether we would be content living our lives over again in exactly the same way. To pass the test of the eternal return, which posits that the lives we now live will be lived innumerable times again in the same manner, down to the smallest detail, we must deem our lives worthy of repeating. If we answer "yes, we would gladly live our lives over again," then we affirm our existence—we have no regrets and do not feel that there is anything lacking in our lives. If the answer is "no, we would reject such a proposition and choose to live differently," then we are not living our best lives and we are not in love with our fates.

Coming to grips with the idea of eternal return, Nietzsche thinks, will awaken us to make the most of our lives and live joyfully. We will seek to take action and create our lives as works of art worthy of imitation. This is how he posits his test: "What, if some day or night a demon were to steal after you in your loneliest loneliness and say to you: 'This life as you now live it and have lived it, you will have to live once more and innumerable times more; and there will be nothing new in it, but every pain and every joy and every thought and sigh and everything unutterably small or great in your life will have to return to you, all in the same succession and sequence'—If this thought gained possession of you, it would change you as you are or perhaps crush you; the question in each and every thing."[135]

Nietzsche's ideas were far ahead of his time, but they may have been too grand even for him. He was aware that the radically independent thinker who stands against the herd "goes voluntarily into a madhouse."[136] At the age of 44, Nietzsche suffered a mental collapse. No one knows the exact cause of his breakdown. Some speculate that he had syphilis. Others say he was driven to madness by his philosophy, and others still that he was pushed to madness by his overbearing mother and sister. The most common story is that Nietzsche witnessed the beating of a horse in the streets of Turin. Running to the horse's aid, he threw his arms around its neck and then fell to the street. An invalid for the rest of his life, he was placed in a sanitarium and then in his family's care. He was never again to return to sanity or philosophizing. But his ideas continue to have an enduring impact. They have given rise to existentialist and postmodern thought. We can imagine Nietzsche philosophizing, or better yet dancing, atop a mountain, for it was in mountain air that Nietzsche thought we could think best. "It should have sung, this 'new soul'—and not spoken!"[137]

# APPLYING NIETZSCHE'S PHILOSOPHY

Nietzsche asks you to affirm your life and live joyfully. Stop tolerating what brings you down and say "yes" to what lifts you up high. It is time for you to own up to who you are, admit your desires, and take action. You don't have to explain yourself or justify your life to anyone. Tune into your instincts: they are the music of your soul. Stop acting in self-defeating ways that diminish your power while enhancing the power of others. Have the courage to be yourself. Know what is to your advantage and act in ways that enhance rather than weaken your authority. Don't allow yourself to be crippled by self-doubt, self-consciousness, or self-criticism. It is in bad taste to always seek reasons behind your actions and feelings. Fight the cultural shame associated with acting to promote your advantage, and trust your instincts. If you judge some of your characteristics to be weak or unattractive, find ways to turn them into strengths and beauty. If you are motivated by destructive instincts, uproot them and replace them with positive instincts. Make the most out of what you have been given. Embrace your unique physical attributes and personality quirks and make them work for you.

Tune into your desires and create the life that brings you joy. Tune out the negativity of self-destructive thinking and the judgement of others. Don't act in ways that make you accept a weaker image of yourself. Prioritize the values that help you build a more affirmative life. The price you pay by striving to fit in is robbing you of your vigor. Shape your life into a work of art and live by your own standards of taste. Discover your strengths and weaknesses and tailor them into a style that promotes your beauty and power. There is no one else like you. Your life should be easy, necessary, and free. Live your life in such a way that you would happily experience it over and over again in exactly the same way for eternity. Ask yourself if you would willing feel all the feelings you have experienced in your life again. Consider, from the perspective of your death, if you would happily and calmly say to yourself that your life was worth it. If you would be upset to repeat your life then take steps to make a change. Work to become who you are and love the fate you have created for yourself. Imagine yourself free, dancing at the edge of your fears, accepting life as it is, uncertain, painful, beautiful, surprising, and the greatest adventure you will ever have.

# QUESTIONS FOR CONSIDERATION

- *Do you know what makes you stronger and what weakens you?*

- *Do your actions and practices enhance your energy and make you feel vigorous, robust, and healthy, or do you act in ways that weaken you and drain your power?*

- *Do you judge yourself according to others' values or your own values?*

- *How would you act if you had no fear, shame, or embarrassment?*

- *Are you carrying any truths and values from your past that are no longer living values for you?*

- *Start a habit of asking yourself before making any choice "Will this weaken or strengthen my sense of power and who I am?"*

- *Have you made a conscious effort to give form and style to your life?*

- *Do you allow your instincts to shape your style?*

- *How can you beautify the things about yourself that you dislike?*

- *Do you affirm your life such that if given the choice you would choose to live your exact same life over again?*

# W. E. B. Du Bois

1868 USA   1963 GHANA

## *Education Opens up the Future*

W.E.B. Du Bois is a philosopher of education. He teaches us to understand the mechanisms involved in our self-perceptions, and to separate the views others have of us from our own views of ourselves. Du Bois was born of African descent into a heritage of enslavement and systematic degradation by White people. He rallied African Americans to fight against deep feelings of shame and low self-esteem. The devastating heritage of slavery had ill prepared the newly freed men and women for independence. This left them with little foundation upon which to build a positive sense of worth. Self-doubt, buttressed by a general disdain and hatred for everything about Black people, plunged African Americans into despair. Yet, in addition to decrying racial injustice, violence, and discrimination, Du Bois cleverly turned the situation around to empower the African American community. He sternly placed the burden of change at their feet by inspiring purpose and education as tools to build self-esteem and feelings of self-worth. Without education, we are likely to get caught up in the ideas others have of us without knowing how these ideas become part of our own self-consciousnesses.

Du Bois asks us to examine the chains that shackle our minds. While Black people had attained freedom from physical slavery, the battle to free themselves from mental slavery had just begun. African Americans had come to freedom in a world that afforded them no means for arriving at their own self-understanding. It rather forced them to think about themselves from the perspective of the White majority. Du Bois calls this "double consciousness" wherein Black people see themselves constantly reflected by "a world which yields him no true self-consciousness, but only lets him see himself through the revelation of the other world."[138] Double consciousness describes how Black people struggle between seeing themselves simultaneously through their own eyes and through the eyes of hateful White people. For centuries, White people had legal control over Black lives, bodies, and the conditions under which they lived—or did not live. "It is a peculiar sensation," Du Bois writes, "this double-consciousness, this sense of always looking at one's self through the eyes of others, of measuring one's soul by the tape of a world that looks on in amused contempt and pity. One ever feels his twoness—an American, a Negro; two souls, two thoughts, two unreconciled strivings; two warring ideals in one dark body, whose dogged strength alone keeps it from being torn asunder." [139]

Du Bois wrote at a time when it was difficult for African Americans to see themselves from a vantage point other than that afforded them by the dominant White world. Double consciousness produces a twoness that battles in the souls of Black people. This twoness renders them incapable of action and at constant war with themselves. Empowering his community with a sense of purpose, Du Bois aimed to merge this "double self into a better and truer and self."[140] Through Black liberation and a study of the conditions of African American existence, African Americans could help the United States bring about its lofty goals of democracy. In so doing, it would finally become a nation of justice and liberty for all. Du Bois taught that African Americans had a mission to make America realize its true potential: "the harbinger of that black tomorrow which is yet destined to soften the whiteness of the Teutonic today."[141] Through the promotion of Black institutions and education, Du Bois inspired African Americans to build character and attain positive self-worth, while adding culture and softness to the rough and materialistic American society. Education allows Black people to define a positive identity for themselves and to understand their strengths through an understanding of their struggles.

As a light-skinned black man growing up in the liberal town of Great Barrington, Massachusetts, Du Bois didn't initially experience the trauma of racism. It was not until grade school, when a newcomer entered the classroom and refused his greeting card that he was first made aware that he was different. His concept of the "veil" characterizes the gap that separates African Americans from the privileged world of White people and "all their dazzling opportunities."[142] Du Bois explains that he could have turned his anger and frustration at injustice back upon himself, as many around him had done. Instead, he devoted himself to learning. He was aware of the gift of "second sight" that the veil afforded him, the gift of seeing the viewpoints of both the oppressed and their White oppressors. After graduating with a doctorate in philosophy from Harvard, the first African American to attain such an honor, Du Bois went on to help found the National Association for the Advancement of Colored People (NAACP) and serve as editor of its journal, *The Crisis*.

Assimilation into an American identity modeled on Whiteness was tempting to those in his community desperate to escape the stigma of Blackness. Yet Du Bois knew that assimilation was not a reality. Black people were free in principle but not in fact. They could not vote, lynching was a daily occurrence, and imprisonment became the new system of slavery. Alert to the tendency to minimize race distinctions to escape from the pressures of being Black in a world designed to "inculcate disdain for everything black," Du Bois drew upon his academic studies and developed a new conception of race to unite his community to make personal and political change.[143] By joining together, African Americans could support each other in building a positive sense of worth and a just American society. "Weighted with a heritage of moral iniquity from our past history, hard pressed in the economic world by foreign immigrants and native prejudice, hated here, despised there and pitied everywhere; our one haven of refuge is ourselves, and but one means of advance, our own belief in our great destiny, our own implicit trust in our ability and worth."[144]

While people have always understood themselves in terms of groups differentiated by land, language, food, and culture, it was not until the seventeenth century that the idea of race originated as a way to categorize people by skin color. Prior to this idea, identities were fluid and changed each time individuals took on new languages and cultures. Skin color was not given much weight. The various tribes in Africa, for example, did not identify as one people based on their skin color, nor did the differing European nations see themselves as unified on the basis of their Whiteness. By the nineteenth century, the idea of race based on skin color had developed further. It was used to classify people into fixed biological categories with the support of spurious scientific studies, such as those which measured skull size. In the American colonies, the idea of race was used to prevent poor White people from joining together with poor Black people to challenge the powerful and wealthy White elite. We now know that there are no biological markers or gene clusters that identify race or which cluster people according to skin color. There is more genetic variation between two people belonging to the same so-called race than there is between those belonging to different racial categories. There is more genetic variation between two Black people than there is between a White and Black person.

To give meaning to Black suffering while providing Black people with a vehicle for spiritual, personal, and political agency, Du Bois introduces his message of the "conservation of races." He recognizes that the idea of race is imbued with deep historical meaning and will not disappear overnight: "a careful consideration of history" will show that "human beings are divided into races."[145] But he does not accept the reigning scientific division of humans into races used to secure White supremacy, nor does he entirely believe that race is a biological necessity. For Du Bois, the force of race is social and historical. He defines race as a type of family or group of people who have shared traditions, histories, languages, and goals. This conception of race allows Du Bois to organize African Americans around a shared project of self-liberation and pride. African Americans are also organized around the important task of liberating the American ideals of freedom and democracy, and enriching American culture. "We are the people whose subtle sense of song has given America its only American music, its only American fairy tales, its only touch of pathos and humor amid its mad money-getting plutocracy. As such, it is our duty to conserve our physical powers, our intellectual endowments, our spiritual ideals; as a race we must strive by race organization, by race solidarity, by race unity to the realization of that broader humanity which freely recognizes differences in men, but sternly deprecates inequality in their opportunities of development."[146]

Du Bois empowers those struggling against oppression to join and build their identities within communities that share the same purpose. He asks us not to see ourselves through the categories into which we are grouped by those in power, but rather to build our own communities through shared struggle. Du Bois calls upon African Americans to make changes to broader society and within themselves by embarking on the project of education. He believed that through self-examination and the study of Black life and the liberal arts, African Americans would expand their horizons. They would understand themselves on their own terms instead of through the prism of White society and White supremacy. He shows us that by investing in ourselves we simultaneously see ourselves as worthy of investment.

Du Bois asks us to take the time to build self-worth and confidence through education. He knew that it would not be easy to enlist Black people into the pursuit of higher learning. Those struggling to survive did not have the leisure or the peace of mind to pursue careful and prolonged study; nor did they have the money and material support. To many, Black and White alike, his call for education seemed no more than a fantastical dream. "Lo! We are diseased and dying, cried the dark hosts; we cannot write, our voting is in vain; what need of education, since we must always cook and serve? And the Nation echoed and enforced this self-criticism, saying Be content to be servants, and nothing more; what need of higher culture for half-men?" [147]

Booker T. Washington, the most influential Black intellectual of the nineteenth century, denounced the idea of a liberal arts education. He called on Black people to cease demanding civil and political equality. Instead, he offered free vocational training at the school he founded in Alabama, the Tuskegee Institute. He believed that learning a trade would lead to employment and the means to economic freedom. Du Bois criticized this program: he argued that a trade education at the cost of a liberal arts education would keep African Americans from developing their full human potential. He characterized Washington's program as "a gospel of Work and Money to such an extent as apparently almost completely to overshadow the higher aims of life."[148] Moreover, Du Bois exclaimed, without political rights Black people would be unable to protect their wealth. They would remain subservient and vulnerable to the whims of White people.

Du Bois was aware that a liberal arts education would be a long and slow process, providing no immediate gratification for many fighting just to stay alive. His call for education was also met by racist pseudoscientific ideas positing that racial traits were fixed and not subject to improvement. But he continued to ask his community to have faith that they would flourish through a commitment to education. In an ideal world, society would pave the way for the formerly enslaved to get on their feet. In the reality of the nineteenth century, it fell upon African Americans to make this difficult journey themselves. "A people thus handicapped," Du Bois writes, "ought not to be asked to race with the world, but rather allowed to give all its time and thought to its own social problems."[149]

Du Bois asks us to trust that change will occur through the journey of education. Fortified by a commitment to our sense of purpose and to self-improvement, education allows us to undergo a metamorphosis. Through this metamorphosis, we may emerge profoundly changed. Most importantly, Du Bois shows us that the gift of education lies in the satisfaction of learning for its own sake. But we must have faith in the process. Du Bois reminds us: "To the tired climbers, the horizon was ever dark, the mists were often cold, the Canaan was always dim and far away. If, however, the vistas disclosed as yet no goal, no resting-place, little but flattery and criticism, the journey at least gave leisure for reflection and self-examination; it changed the child of Emancipation to the youth with dawning self-consciousness, self-realization, self-respect."[150] Devoting time to ourselves and taking time out from the business of life, we undergo a transformation as we work toward developing our minds and expanding our horizon of possibilities. Through this transformation that occurs as we study and learn, we find ourselves. "In those sombre forests of his striving his own soul rose before him, and he saw himself."[151]

Du Bois had devoted his life to fighting against racism. He had watched his first born and only son die at the age of eighteen months while he was teaching in the South. This fate could perhaps have been averted with proper medical care, had the white physicians not refused to treat his black child. After years of being targeted and harassed by the FBI, particularly for his opposition to nuclear weapons and his peace activism, Du Bois was eventually indicted on a charge by the Federal government. Regrettably, the NAACP did not come to his aid, although Albert Einstein offered his support and pledged to appear as a character witness for Du Bois. The case was eventually dismissed, but Du Bois had his passport taken away for eight years.

When Du Bois was able to travel again, he went to Ghana to work on an encyclopedia of the African diaspora funded by the Ghanaian government. When it was time to come home, however, the US government refused to renew his passport. A few months later, Du Bois died in Ghana, just one day before Martin Luther King delivered his "I Have a Dream" speech in Washington, DC. Before King's speech, those at the March were asked to observe a moment of silence to honor Du Bois. He did not live to see the many reforms he had advocated become incorporated into the US Civil Rights Act of 1964.

# APPLYING DU BOIS' PHILOSOPHY

Du Bois wants you to take the time to invest in yourself. You are worth it. Work on self-improvement through education and build your confidence and self-esteem. Begin by understanding the mechanisms involved in your own self-perception and learn to separate the views others have of you from your own positive sense of self. Understand the different forces that shape your self-image and that may have gotten into your self-consciousness while you were young and defenseless. You may be unconsciously or consciously absorbing how others see you through harmful stereotypes and biases. Don't underestimate the impact that people's negative views about you and your abilities may have upon your own self-development and self-understanding.

Identify the barriers that block you from becoming the person you want to be. Guard against looking at yourself through the eyes of others. When you value yourself using the world's tape measure, you prevent yourself from being inventive: and you will always fall short because you cannot be anyone other than yourself. Don't contribute to your feelings of self-doubt by being vulnerable to how others see you. Internalizing other people's perceptions of you will leave you questioning who you are and your place in the world. When you are internally divided, without a strong sense of self, you lack the foundation upon which to chart a course for your future. Believe in your purpose and put the time and effort into educating yourself to achieve your goals. Do not give up because the rewards are not immediately or materially tangible. Education takes time to mature. The power to reinvent yourself will grow out of your struggles to learn what was previously unknown to you. Don't run from your history, or try to change yourself to fit into what is valued by the dominant culture. Your history has a lot to teach you, and you will always find things that you are proud of. Seek support from others who are going through similar struggles and who face the same set of oppositions as you do. You have the power to overcome oppression and realize a positive sense of worth through education.

# QUESTIONS FOR CONSIDERATION

- *Are you at war with yourself, battling between who you are and who others think you should be?*

- *Can you identify when you are of two minds about something, and what factors are at play?*

- *Are you able to hear your own voice, or do you internalize other people's ideas of who you are?*

- *What do you tell yourself that may be holding you back from achieving your goals?*

- *How do you allow social categories and expectations to define who you are?*

- *What values have you adopted that make you feel less than worthy?*

- *What ideas and values would make you have a positive image of yourself?*

- *Are you in supportive communities?*

- *Do you try to fit into groups that you might be better off leaving?*

- *Are you trying to escape from your history because it is too painful or a source of shame?*

- *Do you take time to better yourself through education and practices that work toward your self-improvement?*

# Simone Weil

1909 FRANCE    1943 UNITED KINGDOM

## *Attention Is the Rarest and Purest Form of Generosity*

Simone Weil is a philosopher of attention. She asks us to give our attention to what feeds the soul and supports the human spirit. Weil believes the most loving thing we can do for others is to listen and see them without distraction by giving them our concentrated attention. For Weil, attention is a disposition: it is a way of being toward others in generosity, love, and prayer. "Attention is the rarest and purest form of generosity."[152] When we are distracted, we relate to others from our self-interest or ego: we are therefore not giving the other person our undivided attention. When we are truly and fully present for the other, we stand in true attention. Weil describes attention as "suspending our thought, leaving it detached, empty, and ready to be penetrated by the object … Above all our thought should be empty, waiting, not seeking anything, but ready to receive in its naked truth the object that is to penetrate it."[153]

Weil asks us to see others in the generosity of loving attention. In attention, we obligate ourselves to meet the physical and spiritual needs of others. Attention is a bestowal of existence and recognition upon the other. Loving attention is compassionate awareness. To give others our attention we must suspend the ego and rise above its limits to allow others to impress us and take us into their lives. "The love of our neighbor in all its fullness simply means being able to say, 'What are you going through?'" When we are generous in our attention, we are receptive to others in their truth. We can approach what Weil calls the "impersonal" and "anonymous" in them. The impersonal is that which is sacred and holy in all of us. Seeing others as raw, rather than defined by their circumstances, is to see them without preference or prejudice: to see them through the impersonal. The generosity of attention is not given to this or that individual as they are defined in society, but to all humans in their vulnerability and fragility. This fragility is the impersonal and anonymous that is the mark of the human spirit. Weil explains: "Neither the person nor the human person in him or her is holy to me . . . Far from it: it is that which is impersonal in a human being. All that is impersonal in humankind is holy, and that alone."[154]

Weil directs our sights toward the divine. In attention to the impersonal, we receive others in their truth without the limitations of our egos. For Weil, the most direct route to the impersonal is through acknowledgement of the deep suffering of what she calls "affliction." An emphasis on progress, success, wealth, and youth shields us from the vulnerability of the human condition. Focused on material rewards, we seek to expand rather than retract our egos. We cover up the impersonal that unites us to the holy. Through attention to affliction, we see others as they are and bear witness to the injustice and suffering in the world. Informed by her voluntary work in factories and on farms, Weil conceived her notion of affliction after observing the exploitation, humiliation, and dehumanization of the poor. Those who are worn-down, oppressed, and powerless suffer in all aspects of their existence. This deep suffering of affliction is different from simple suffering: it uproots lives and guts the soul. "Just as truth is a different thing than opinion, so affliction is a different thing than suffering," Weil writes. "Affliction is a device for pulverizing the soul; the man who falls into it is like a workman who gets caught up in a machine. He is no longer a man but a torn and bloody rag on a cog-wheel."[155]

Weil asks us to find our way back to the spiritual and mysterious side of life by existing between love and despair. When we are victims of violence, when we have our loved ones taken from us through unspeakable acts of brutality, or when we witness others perish before our eyes, we stand in the face of affliction. Affliction leaves us without a sense of security and robs the world of any order it once had. When affliction strikes, it takes possession of our souls: it radically and permanently alters our social, psychological, and physical well-being. At first a Marxist, Weil came to believe that the true opiate of the masses was not religion but revolution. Those who are humiliated, dehumanized, and beaten down in affliction are not primed for rebellion. They are instead fatigued, submissive, and hopeless. In affliction we encounter the void. "Chief use of suffering which is to teach me that I am nothing."[156] In this void where we are stripped of self lies the possibility of penetrating others in their truth and also of communicating with divinity. Weil writes: "The soul empties itself [*se vide*] of all its own contents in order to receive into itself the being it is looking at, just as he is, in all his truth. Only he who is capable of attention can do this."[157]

Weil meets this void of affliction with the generosity and compassion of attention. She asks us to harness the eternal and the impersonal by emptying ourselves of our egos. When we allow ourselves to be disturbed by the affliction and deep suffering of others, we see and hear them through attention. By diminishing and decentering ourselves we give existence to the other.

But this is not an easy task. The capacity to give one's attention to a sufferer," Weil states, "is a very rare and difficult thing; it is almost a miracle; it is a miracle. Nearly all those who think they have the capacity do not possess it."[158] The greater the suffering, the harder it is for us to attend to the other and bear witness to their pain. As Weil remarks, "Thought revolts from contemplating affliction, to the same degree that living flesh recoils from death."[159] This is why she understands attention to be a form of prayer: "Attention, taken to its highest degree, is the same thing as prayer. It presupposes faith and love."[160]

We are receptive to others and to their pain, humiliation, loss, and affliction when we occupy the void. In the absences that open up when we cease focusing on ourselves, we become vulnerable and see others in their vulnerability. Weil asks us to not rush to fill this void where we encounter the impersonal, but rather to hold the space open for love to fill our beings: "All the natural movements of the soul are controlled by laws analogous to those of physical gravity. Grace is the only exception. Grace fills empty spaces, but it can only enter where there is a void to receive it, and it is grace itself which makes this void."[161] The grace she speaks of is God's love. Without God's love for us, Weil thinks we would not have a motive to love ourselves. "God's love for us is not the reason for which we should love him. God's love for us is the reason for us to love ourselves. How could we love ourselves without this motive?"[162]

Weil approaches philosophy through her unique form of Christianity. Born into a wealthy Parisian secular Jewish family, Weil had a spiritual awakening in her early twenties. She chose not to be baptized into Christianity, as she saw as much truth in ancient Egyptian, Greek, Chinese, and Indian spiritualities. Nor did she join any Church, because of what she considered to be their violent histories and corruption by power. In her version of Christianity, God created the world and then retreated to make room for us. "De-creation" is the term she uses to describe God's act of limiting Himself to create space for His creation and for love. She characterizes this space as the distance between God and Himself—a distance within which life and love unfold. We are at our holiest in de-creation when we imitate God's denial of power for the sake of others and empty ourselves of ego and the desire for self-expansion. In the absence of our egos, we occupy a void and consent to the distance created by God. This is so we may love others in affliction and attention. "The representation of what is unbearable . . . dragging horror out of the gloomy depths and placing it under the light of the attention. It is an act of de-creation."[163]

For Weil, love is found in the distance between God, on the one hand, and God's love of His creation and His own self, on the other. This distance characterizes the void within us: the void that allows us to open ourselves to others in attention. "To love purely is to consent to distance, it is to adore the distance between ourselves and that which we love."[164] When we relinquish our egos to create a distance between ourselves and others, we make space to receive others as they are in their truth and in their affliction. Allowing for distance is the medium and possibility by which we connect to others and to the divine. In this distance wherein we are empty of ego, we stand as a point between God and Himself. We are then able to channel His love, as love traverses the distance between God and Himself, and His creation. It is not a particular individual who loves, but "it is God in us who loves them [les malheureux]."[165] God's love powers human love through the distance we create for others to approach us in their truth. Weil provides the analogy of a wall that spans the distance between God and His creation. This analogy shows how it is that we may stand as a point in the middle of this distance to absorb God's love. While the wall divides us, it is also the impasse by means of which we may communicate with the divine. "Two prisoners whose cells adjoin communicate with each other by knocking on the wall. The wall is the thing which separates them but it is also their means of communication. It is the same with us and God. Every separation is a link."[166]

Weil lived her philosophy relentlessly and with an unfathomable degree of passion. In solidarity with society's poor, she vowed to live as they lived. In the hospital where she fought tuberculosis, she allowed herself to eat only the rations provided to soldiers and those suffering from the food shortage in France. She never made it out of the hospital, dying at the age of thirty-four. The coroner's report listed Weil's cause of death as self-inflicted starvation occurring while her mind was out of balance. But to view Weil's death as a form of suicide or insanity is to do her an injustice by assuming to know her motives. This fails to honor the impersonal in her. We may imagine Weil directing this statement toward those who view her final actions as unstable. "Justice. To be ever ready to admit that another person is something quite different from what we read when he is there (or when we think about him). Or rather, to read in him that he is certainly something different, perhaps something completely different from what we read in him. Every being cries out silently to be read differently."[167]

Acknowledging her passion, rebellion, and resilience, Albert Camus declared that "Weil was the only great spirit of our time." He went on to edit and publish much of her work on politics and philosophy, and was profoundly influenced by her thought. Camus also stopped at her home in Stockholm to meditate before receiving his Nobel Prize in Literature. For Weil, attention to suffering is what unites us with the divine. Through the weight of the gravity of life we are drawn upward by grace through the act of attention where we give existence to the other by diminishing and de-centering ourselves.

# APPLYING WEIL'S PHILOSOPHY

Weil wants you to empty yourself of ego so that you can be sensitive to the pain and vulnerability of human suffering. Slavery, exploitation, war, dehumanizing and humiliating work, are all marks of the deep suffering she calls affliction. Suffering from violence, hatred, poverty, discrimination and dislocation is all around you. Find your way back to the holy and the sacred by allowing yourself to be disturbed by the suffering of others. Let down your defenses to see into those who are broken and powerless. When you encounter yourself and others as fragile and vulnerabile, you approach the holy that lies within each of us. Open yourself to the suffering of others through the generosity and compassion of attention. In attention you meet the void of suffering and are raw and ripe to be possessed by the world of spirit.

Give others your full and undivided attention, and do not be desensitized to their pain. Attention is an obligation to be present, by which you bestow existence and recognition upon the other. The greater the suffering, the harder it will be for you to attend to the other and bear witness to their pain. Meet the agony of suffering that characterizes the impersonal in all of us with compassionate attention. The impersonal is the part of you that you share with everyone else by virtue of being human and vulnerable. The impersonal is the anonymous self that is stripped of all social rankings. Stop relating to others through greed, self-interest, and fear, and focus instead on their care. Caring for others is how you regain your connection to the spiritual and mysterious aspects of life. Don't be distracted when you are with others. You can bestow loving attention onto others by asking them how they are doing and generously listening to them.

# QUESTIONS FOR CONSIDERATION

- *What shields do you use that prevent you from acknowledging your own and others' vulnerability, suffering, and fragility?*

- *Have you ever experienced the rawness and humility of being broken?*

- *Are you aware that there are people living in fear, domination, and bondage that call out to be seen by you?*

- *Are you able to honor the pain and suffering of others and approach them through loving compassion?*

- *Have you ever been transformed by witnessing another person's pain and suffering?*

- *Are you distracted when you are with others, and what means of distraction do you employ that prevent you from giving them your undivided attention?*

- *Do you allow others to see you in your fragility and vulnerability, free of masks and pretenses?*

- *How would you treat yourself and others differently if you accepted the fragility that marks the human condition?*

- *Are you able to see the impersonal and holy in others by seeing beyond the particularities of their everyday existence to greet them with compassion?*

- *What would you need to do to bestow attention on others and allow them the space to show themselves to you completely?*

- *Are you able to give others your complete and undivided attention and see this as a form of love and generosity?*

# Hannah Arendt

1906 GERMANY    1975 USA

## *There Are No Dangerous Thoughts Thinking Itself Is Dangerous*

Hannah Arendt is a philosopher of thinking. She coined the term "banality of evil"[168] to explain how it is possible for ordinary people to commit horrible atrocities without much thought. Indeed, it is precisely because of what she calls "thoughtlessness" that we are capable of engaging in evil acts. Before Arendt, it was common to think of evil as a kind of demonic possession, temporary insanity, a weakness of will, or the consequence of passion—jealousy, greed, hate, or envy. More importantly, evil acts were believed to be accompanied by evil motives. Arendt's notion of evil breaks radically with this history: she roots evil in a commonplace lack of critical thinking. She finds that few of us have the resources to resist authority because few of us exercise our ability to think independently. To resist evil, she asks us to engage vigilantly in the practice of independent thought, reflection, and judgment— what Arendt calls "thinking without a banister."[169] Thinking is how we live in peace and openness with ourselves through inner dialogue. "The presupposition for this kind of judging is not a highly developed intelligence or sophistication in moral matters, but merely the habit of living together explicitly with oneself, that is, of being engaged in that silent dialogue between me and myself which since Socrates and Plato we usually call thinking."[170]

Arendt arrived at her conception of evil while on an assignment in Jerusalem for the New Yorker magazine. Sent there to cover the trial of accused Nazi war criminal Adolf Eichmann, she had hoped to gain insight into the conditions that had made possible the Holocaust against Jews and the killing of Roma, communists, gays, and other undesirables in Germany. She tried to understand how a society could abandon their old moral customs and submit to a new standard of morality—and do so without debate, questioning, or much opposition. Eichmann, a Lieutenant Colonel, had been charged with overseeing the deportation of Jews and other so-called degenerates to concentration camps. Before entering the courtroom, Arendt had imagined she would see evil incarnate in Eichmann. But, to her surprise, Eichmann appeared as a simple and ordinary man. It was this alarming normality that suggested to Arendt that evil is not exceptional, but more commonplace than generally assumed.

Listening to Eichmann defend his participation in the Holocaust, Arendt was struck by the lack of intent behind his actions. He claimed to have harbored no ill will or hatred toward Jews that the Nazis had wished to remove from German society. To the contrary, he repeatedly declared that he had many reasons to like Jews, and counted them among his friends. Rather, Eichmann was a simple bureaucrat. Following orders, his objective was only to advance his career, which Arendt notes, is not itself a crime. What motivated Eichmann, she argues, was petty ambition and basic self-interest. In this, Eichmann was by no means exceptional, but quite ordinary and mediocre. This was what Arendt found so disconcerting. "The trouble with Eichmann was precisely that so many were like him, and that the many were neither perverted nor sadistic, that they were, and still are terribly and terrifyingly normal."[171]

Arendt wants us to take thinking seriously as a moral and political task. She asks us to consider the consequences of our actions so that we can live in peace with ourselves. The less we reflect on our ideas and beliefs, the more likely we are to be overcome by the influences of authority. She observes how Eichmann acted routinely and without motive in executing his task to rid Germany of those deemed dangerous to the soul of the nation. Hiding behind a storehouse of stock phrases provided by the German Empire, it simply never occurred to Eichmann to question authority, or think about his actions. He was just doing his job. Because he was going with the grain of German society, he did not think he was participating in anything evil. To the contrary, in agreement with the crowd he thought of himself as a law-abiding citizen. He would have felt himself to be defiant and insubordinate had he gone against the judgment of his superiors and community. "His conscience was indeed set at rest when he saw the zeal and eagerness which 'good society' everywhere reacted as he did. He did not need to 'close his ears to the voice of conscience,' as the judgment has it, not because he had none, but because his conscience spoke with a 'respectable voice,' with the voice of respectable society around him."[172] Who was he to judge, Eichmann had asked himself. "'Who was he to have [his] own thoughts in the matter?'"[173] To further ease his conscience, Eichmann pointed out that many Jews aided the Nazis' administrative and police work. Without their help, he claimed, the Nazis' mission would not have been as efficient.

Acting in conformity with members of his community, Eichmann was unaware of his own wickedness. He could easily say to himself that he had not committed atrocities, but had acted according to orders. If anything, he believed he had been made to endure atrocities to accomplish his duties. The evil in his actions was complicit with his thoughtlessness: "He would have had a bad conscience only if he had not done what he had been ordered to—to ship millions of men, women, and children to their death with great zeal and the most meticulous care."[174] Arendt controversially concludes that evil is not rooted in wicked intentions, but rather in the commonplace failure to think independently and engage in thoughtful reflection. "There was no sign in him of ideological convictions or of specific evil motives, and the only notable characteristic one could detect in his past behavior as well as in his behavior during the trial . . . was something entirely negative: it was not stupidity but *thoughtlessness*."[175]

The banality of evil suggests that evil is not extraordinary. Even ordinary people, corruptible by self-interest or shallowness, are capable of horrendous behavior when they fail to think for themselves. What characterizes Eichmanns everywhere is their absence of independent critical thinking. Thinking requires depth. It demands that we look at a matter in all its uniqueness and particularity. Entertaining different perspectives, we can penetrate beyond shallowness and fixed notions of reality to look at each situation in its singularity. This is how thinking shields us from the control of others and allows new perspectives to arise. For Arendt, the contrary of thinking is fanaticism. "To hold different opinions and to be aware that other people think differently on the same issue shields us from Godlike certainty which stops all discussion and reduces social relationships to those of an ant heap. A unanimous public opinion tends to eliminate bodily those who differ, for mass unanimity is not the result of agreement, but an expression of fanaticism and hysteria."[176]

Arendt dares us to think for ourselves and be mindful of the particularities of each situation we encounter. She asks us to consider, before we act, if we would be able to live with ourselves after committing certain deeds. Arendt believes that we are all susceptible to evil if we do not defend against it by exercising independent thought. Thinking demands courage. Ironically, Arendt paid a severe price for thinking without a banister. She was vilified as an Eichmann sympathizer and a self-hating Jew for revealing the extent of Jewish collaboration with the Nazis and for not labeling Eichmann as an extremist who engaged in unique crimes against Jews. The attacks against her were so ferocious that her close friend, the writer Mary McCarthy, described them as reaching "the proportions of a pogrom."[177] Made a pariah in her own community and shunned by her closest friends, Arendt suffered dearly for using her mind. Yet, Arendt resisted the pressures of her critics and stood by her conclusions so that she may live in peace with herself. For Arendt, evil is banal and more commonplace than we would like to believe. Unless we think for ourselves, we risk getting caught up in crimes against humanity.

# APPLYING ARENDT'S PHILOSOPHY

Arendt wants you to think for yourself and come to your own conclusions. Use your own judgment and seek out your own information. Be careful not to blindly follow authority or the opinion of others. Thinking is not solely an intellectual exercise, but the most significant factor in ethical and civic behavior. Do not evade responsibility by deferring to those deemed experts, or to politically popular perspectives to tell you what to do. You cannot hide from the effects of your actions by claiming you were simply obeying orders, or just doing what everyone else was doing. Unquestioningly following orders or accepting the judgment of others, you do not converse with yourself, and therefore you do not think. Arendt calls this "thoughtlessness." When you fail to exercise independent thought, you become vulnerable to the conformity and safety of following with the crowd, and are likely to cause harm to others. Ask yourself before acting if you could live with yourself after committing certain deeds. If you can reconcile your actions with your conscience, then you will be able to live in peace with yourself.

Don't allow your comfort, convenience, or self-interest to shield you from thinking about the consequences of your actions. Recognize that your responsibility to others is dependent on your ability to arrive at your own judgments. Listening to others and entertaining different opinions is only possible if you allow yourself to think from a variety of perspectives. Break free from prejudices. They close your mind by confining it to seeing in generalities that prevent you from recognizing the particularities of a situation. Expand your mind and let your thinking carry you toward unknown horizons. In this space of the unknown you can encounter others in their difference, and open yourself up to their viewpoints. Every moment has the potential for a fresh beginning if you look at it in its particularity. Each person you meet may introduce you to the unexpected. You have never been in this moment before, so let your thinking be the portal to new possibilities.

# QUESTIONS FOR CONSIDERATION

- *Do you abdicate the responsibility of thinking for yourself by unquestioningly following the advice of people in authority?*

- *Do you now regret any actions that resulted from trying to fit in or conform to the crowd?*

- *Do you sometimes do things that you know are wrong, to be accepted by those whose favor you wish to court?*

- *Do you sometimes act on the basis of self-interest against what you know is right?*

- *Do you close your mind to ideas that do not fit into your world view without reflecting on them?*

- *Do you actively challenge your beliefs and consider ideas from a variety of perspectives?*

- *Have you sometimes failed to see the uniqueness of a situation because you were viewing it through habitual frameworks or prejudices?*

- *Do you allow yourself to come to your own conclusions based on conversations you have with yourself?*

- *Do you think through the consequences that your actions might have on others?*

- *Have you considered how you may be contributing to the suffering of others by allowing your comfort to shield you from thinking about them?*

- *Do you consider how your actions may indirectly be contributing to the suffering of others, or how you may be benefiting from other people's suffering?*

# Jean-Paul Sartre

1905 FRANCE   1980 FRANCE

## *There Is No Reality Except in Action*

Jean-Paul Sartre is a philosopher of action. In Sartre's conception of life, there is no creator or underlying nature shaping our existence. There is no fate or destiny, no true self that needs to be unearthed or expressed, and no divine plan for our lives to follow. There is only choice, and the lives we create for ourselves by way of our freedom and actions. Sartre depicts the weight of existential choice in his paradoxical assertion that "man is condemned to be free."[178] We are so condemned because whether or not we acknowledge and accept it, we are sentenced to bear the full weight of responsibility for the lives we have created through our choices. There are indeed facts about us, such as the place and time of our birth, the nation and family we are born into, and the historical circumstances into which we are thrown, which Sartre calls "facticity." However, these facts are subject to our interpretations and change through the course of our actions. For Sartre, we are never defined once and for all. Our lives are works in progress: we are always free to change them and give ourselves a new direction with every choice and action we take. As Sartre puts it, "Man is nothing else than his plan; he exists only to the extent that he fulfills himself; he is therefore nothing more than the ensemble of his acts, nothing else than his life."[179]

Sartre unhinges the individual from every determining factor and roots existence squarely in individual choice and action. He quotes the Russian writer Dostoevsky as having once said that if God did not exist, everything would be permitted. For Dostoevsky, having no divine guidance was a cause for concern, but Sartre greets this idea with excitement. No longer do we rely on God or anyone or anything to give our lives meaning. There are no standard values to guide our actions. We are free to make of our lives what we wish. Our lives are entirely defined by our actions and the values we choose to live by, and each of us is fully responsible for the life they have chosen to live. Even the refusal to make a choice is itself a choice to have things remain the same or to have others make decisions for us. It is impossible to escape choice. Sartre's ideas of radical freedom, choice, and responsibility define the modern school of thought called existentialism.

Sartre summarizes his version of existential choice in the statement that "existence is prior to essence."[180] By contrast, a manufactured object such as a paper cutter has its essence determined for it. The paper cutter exists only on account of an artisan who conceives the idea of how to make and use the cutter. Its essence, the idea of what a paper cutter is, precedes its existence. When we deem God as our creator, we say that He, like the artisan behind the paper cutter, is the author of our existence and that our lives follow His plan. Even non-religious notions of human nature posit an essence that we believe give shape to a person's life: when we deem a person to be impulsive by nature, for example. To say instead, like Sartre, that existence precedes essence means that at first we are nothing—we are not defined by any essence. Only later, through our actions, do we become something. "If man, as the existentialist conceives him, is indefinable, it is because at first he is nothing. Only afterward will he be something, and he himself will have made what he will be."[181]

For Sartre, life does not come with instructions or a blueprint. We have to figure out who we want to be and create the kind of life we want to live for ourselves. He warns us against banking on the future of our hopes and dreams. Dreams are nothing but unrealized projects unless we turn them into reality through action. There are no excuses, and no one is to blame for how our lives turn out but ourselves. It may not be a surprise to hear that Sartre's version of radical freedom has been criticized by those who believe his philosophy promotes a form of egoism that leaves too much to the selfish whims of the individual. Without the conception of God or fixed moral values to anchor action, they argue, human life would be arbitrary, negative, devoid of meaning, and lacking a foundation. Sartre counters these objections by describing his existentialism as an optimism, for it asserts that life is an ongoing project that is shaped through our choices.

Sartre suspects that critics of existentialism are afraid to take responsibility for what are likely disappointing and unhappy lives, and that they wish instead to blame someone else or some innate cause for their misery. For some, the burden of responsibility for how one's life turns out is daunting. They may prefer to think, for example, that a coward or a hero is simply born that way. But for Sartre it is never too late for a coward to become a hero. Cowardliness is not an essence that one is born with, or a quality that adheres to someone permanently. Rather, a coward is something we make of ourselves by acting in cowardly ways, and we are free at any moment to change and begin to act heroically. At the heart of these criticisms, Sartre believes, is a fear of freedom and the anxiety that accompanies all major decisions whose outcomes are uncertain. "Can it be that what really scares them in this doctrine I shall try to present here is that it leaves to man a possibility of choice?"[182]

We are the sole authors and creators of our lives. In Sartre's brand of existentialism there are no external supports or aids. We are nothing more than what we make of ourselves, and we are entirely responsible for the lives that we have built through our choices. As Sartre writes, "What man needs is to find himself again and to understand that nothing can save him from himself."[183] It is always possible to change our lives. We are works in progress and are never doomed to remain the same. For those who want to blame their circumstances or other people for how their lives turn out, Sartre's philosophy is discomforting. To someone lamenting that they could have become a great musician, for example, had their mother not become sick and in need of their care, Sartre responds by reminding them that there is no reality behind unfulfilled dreams. Who we are is defined by the lives we are living, and the lives we live define who we are and the values we hold most deeply.

Sartre provides an illustration of how our choices define our values in his discussion of a young student who had to decide either to go to England and fight with the Free French Forces, or to stay home to take care of his mother. German soldiers had killed his brother, and he was very eager to avenge his brother's death. Yet he knew his mother lived solely for him, and he alone was concerned for her care. Who or what could help him decide what action to take, Sartre asks? Christian doctrine says to "love thy neighbor." But who was his neighbor: his mother or his fellow French citizens? Sartre's student turned to him and explained he would let his intuition decide, declaring: "in the end it is feeling that counts."[184] But how does one estimate the strength of a feeling? For Sartre, there is no inherent meaning to a feeling. Feelings are vague and indeterminate, acquiring meaning only in their expression through action. A situation may elicit anger in some and not in others. Only after it has been expressed through the act of anger may we identify the feeling as anger. As Sartre reminds us, "There is no reality except in action."[185] The student decided to stay with his mother and in that choice demonstrated that caring for his mother was more important to him than fighting in the war.

Sartre wants us to realize that the lives we are living are the lives that we deem most worthy of living, whether we know it or not. How we live our lives testifies to the values that we hold dear and think are important. "To choose between this or that is at the same time to affirm the value of that which has been chosen," Sartre writes.[186] Nevertheless, he thinks many of us flee from radical freedom into bad faith (*mauvaise foi*)—vacillating between an awareness of our freedom and fleeing from it. We engage in bad faith, translated as self-deception, by believing we are without options, or that our choices have already been determined for us. In bad faith, we may blame others or bad luck for how our lives unfold. More commonly, we simply fail to choose at all and just let life happen to us.

To underscore the idea that we are responsible for the choices we make in creating our lives, Sartre challenges the notion that life may be guided by any kind of sign. He gives an example of a Jesuit who deems his many failed attempts at secular life to be a sign from God to enter religious life. Yet from the outside, we can imagine that he could have interpreted his failures in a variety of different ways. Sartre's point is that if we act based on a sign, it is we who have chosen to give a sign a particular meaning in our lives. If we act on the basis of advice given to us by a friend, it is we who have chosen that particular friend rather than another to turn to for advice, likely already knowing the values they might draw upon to advise us. There is simply no escaping choice.

Sartre asks us to actively choose our lives and assume full responsibility for giving them meaning. For him, there is nothing that defines us at birth or saves us at death. Meaning is not something we discover by retreating within ourselves, but something we create through our actions and the choices we make in the external world. Reluctantly, Sartre chose to be the first person to reject the prestigious Nobel Prize in Literature. Upon hearing he was a contender for the award, he sent a letter asking the committee to remove his name from the list of nominees. He did not want to give any governing body the power to decide the value of his work. He also did not want to be identified with an institution that he felt unfairly favored Western writers. Sartre did not want to be linked to any institution at all, having previously turned down the French Legion of Honor for his military service during the Second World War. The committee gave Sartre the award nevertheless, even though he refused it. At the Nobel banquet in his honor that he did not attend, the emcee tried to make sense of Sartre's refusal of the prize. S. Friberg believed that Sartre's decision to reject the prestigious award stemmed from his commitment to live according to his own principles. In his tribute to Sartre, Friberg ended his speech with a quotation by Ralph Waldo Emerson: "Nothing is at last sacred but the integrity of your own mind."[187]

# APPLYING SARTRE'S PHILOSOPHY

Sartre challenges you to create the life you want to live, not once and for all, but on an ongoing basis. You alone are the author of your life. Through your actions, you give your life meaning and assert what you think is important. Sartre is not troubled by questions like "What is the real me?", "What is the authentic life I am supposed to live?", or "What is my truth?" For him, there is no real you waiting to be found and expressed. You do not have an inborn essence or nature. There is nothing to find by going deeply within, no personal truth that waits to be uncovered. The only truths that exist are the ones that you create through your choices and actions. You are totally free to become the person you want to be, and you are fully responsible for the person you have become through your choices. If your life is not going in the direction you imagine, you have only yourself to blame. You can change your life at any moment because your life is your own creation. You cannot explain your actions by chalking them up to human nature, your upbringing, other people's advice, or your uncontrollable passions. You will find no excuses for your melancholies, miseries, successes, or failures. Your life is a product of your choices and actions and nothing more.

Sartre does not ask you to dig deep and discover who you are. He tells you to act and create the life you want to live. Even making no choice is to choose to keep things as they are, or to have others make choices for you. Freedom is a burden and a responsibility because it means that there is no one to blame for how your life turns out but yourself. You act in what Sartre calls "bad faith" when you declare defeat by proclaiming "this is simply who I am," or "this is simply the way it is; I can't do anything about it." These explanations deny both your freedom and the fact that you are a work in progress. You must own your life and take complete responsibility for your choices. You are never stuck. Seek out alternatives if you are not happy with the way things are. Make choices that speak to your values and the life you find meaningful: don't look for signs to tell you how to live or to others to make decisions for you. Your destiny lies in your own hands. There are no do overs. Choose your own life. Don't let life choose for you.

# QUESTIONS FOR CONSIDERATION

- *Are you aware that you are free to create the life you want?*

- *Are you living the life you would choose to live, or are you afraid to make choices for fear of uncertain outcomes?*

- *Do you believe that your choices define who you are?*

- *Do you believe that you can turn over a new leaf and live differently at any moment by changing your actions?*

- *Are you taking full responsibility for the life you are living and the choices you are making?*

- *How can you overcome the thoughts and circumstances that make you feel trapped and powerless?*

- *Where do you feel stuck?*

- *Can you name a time that you have acted to make a radical change in your life?*

- *Are there any past events that you let determine your future?*

- *Do you let life happen to you as if you are a character in someone else's drama?*

- *Do you blame others for how your life is turning out, or for your circumstances?*

- *How have you given meaning to your life?*

# Simone de Beauvoir

1908 FRANCE   1986 FRANCE

## *To Will Oneself Free Is Also to Will Others Free*

Simone de Beauvoir is a philosopher of ethical freedom. She teaches us to understand freedom as a way to open new worlds for ourselves and others. For de Beauvoir, freedom is not doing what we want when we want. Freedom is the ability to cast ourselves out into an open future rich with possibilities. And because we are always in the world with others, she conceives of individual freedom as inseparably bound by the freedom and liberation of others. Others set the stage for our actions: likewise, we provide others with a world within which to act. We do not create ourselves from nothing. Our freedom is always unfolding within a web of relations with others. "To be free is not to have the power to do anything you like; it is to be able to surpass the given toward an open future; the existence of others as a freedom defines my situation and is even the condition of my own freedom."[188]

De Beauvoir fundamentally believes that the world is ambiguous and unpredictable, gaining its meaning only through human action: "man fulfills himself within the transitory or not at all."[189] Because our actions depend on the actions of others and unfold in an unpredictable world with unknown consequences, de Beauvoir rejects any ethics that provides universal principles or hard and fast rules. She asks us to embrace our freedom within an "ethics of ambiguity." Accepting ambiguity, we act not to accomplish any concrete goal, but simply in our freedom to keep the horizon rich with possibilities. For de Beauvoir, freedom aims only at itself—"an end which is nothing else but precisely the free movement of existence."[190] In de Beauvoir's ethics of freedom and ambiguity, the principle of action is simply to open horizons and multiply possibilities. Keeping horizons open rather than closing them by seeing the world through the prisms of preconceived ideas is how we engage in an ethics of ambiguity. We might recast de Beauvoir's idea of moral freedom as a Kantian categorical imperative: act in such a way that you promote your future and the future of others by keeping possibilities open.

De Beauvoir is acutely aware that certain groups have fewer choices than others. She is best known for challenging the sexist oppression that robs women of their freedom and ultimately robs society of women's contributions. In *The Second Sex* (1949) she examines the historical dynamics of women's oppression and the cultural channels by which the sexed female body is socially transformed through the learning and practice of feminine behaviors, sentiments, and expectations. De Beauvoir identifies these social practices as gender roles, as opposed to roles defined by our biological sex. Gender roles are neither natural nor innate, but are culturally determined. In a key statement, de Beauvoir asserts that "One is not born, but rather becomes a woman."[191] Biological differences do not, for example, determine that pink is better suited for a girl than is blue. Gender does that. Gender expectations, defined by societal norms, dictate culturally appropriate behaviors and roles for men and women to play. De Beauvoir recognizes that there are deeply ingrained internal and external barriers that inhibit the oppressed from actualizing their freedom. However, she also points out that some of us hide from freedom. We choose the safety of fixed roles to protect ourselves from the ambiguity and uncertainty of existence. In hiding behind traditionally given roles, we not only escape our own freedom but also fail to promote freedom and possibility in the world at large.

De Beauvoir asks us to keep the future open by embracing ambiguity and recognizing others in their freedom and difference. We should always leave room for the unexpected and uncertain. It is in our encounters with the unknown where freedom is most at home. "Man must not attempt to dispel the ambiguity of his being but, on the contrary, accept the task of realizing it."[192] She warns against subsuming our freedom toward any concrete goal or identity. We do not act in freedom if our actions are framed by fixed identities or political ideals representative of a certain party line, for instance. We do not act in freedom when we hide behind a movement, or even a passion toward which we dedicate our lives. When we direct our freedom toward concrete ends, we close off possibilities and act as one who "bars the horizon and bolts the sky."[193] Certainty closes off possibilities. It is the enemy of freedom, leading to oppression and domination. Certainty fears ambiguity.

Like her romantic and philosophical partner Jean-Paul Sartre, de Beauvoir believes we are free to create our own lives and must bear full responsibility for the meaning we give to them. But unlike Sartre, who sees others as potential challenges to our freedom, de Beauvoir embraces the other. In de Beauvoir's existentialist ethics our lives are necessarily intertwined with the freedom of others. Our actions impact the possibility of others' actions: other people's actions likewise impact our access to opportunities. "No existence is fulfilled without appeal to the existence of others."[194] We are thrown into a world left behind by others. In our concern for others, we shape how the world opens up for us and for them. This is why she teaches us that if we want to live freely, we must ensure that others are also free. It is ultimately others who provide the conditions for our own freedom: "To will oneself free is also to will others free."[195]

We keep the future open by recognizing others in their freedom and difference. It is in the interest of freedom to keep horizons open. Unless all are free, de Beauvoir thinks that none of us is truly free. When others are oppressed, freedom is compromised for all of us: the conditions of freedom are suspended not only for them but also for us. De Beauvoir therefore believes we must fight for the liberation of others, admonishing us that "abstention is complicity."[196] We are responsible for protecting the other from becoming an object of our will or another's. We must not limit the freedom of others by objectifying them or fixing them into certain roles. Presuming to know the other rather than recognizing them in their difference is to rob them of their freedom to create meaning for themselves. Presuming to know the other, we also rob ourselves of developing and growing in relation to the unexpected possibilities that others offer us. "As we have seen, my freedom, in order to fulfill itself, requires that it emerge into an open future: it is other men who open the future to me, it is they who, setting up the world of tomorrow, define my future; but if . . . they keep me below the level which they have conquered and on the basis of which new conquests will be achieved, then they are cutting me off from the future, they are changing me into a thing."[197]

De Beauvoir teaches us that ultimately love is the engine of freedom. Love is how we let the other be who they are: "Love is then renunciation of all possession, of all confusion. One renounces being in order that there may be that being which one is not."[198] Love opens a space for others to act in freedom independently of our control and expectations. This is why de Beauvoir asks us to question and examine our actions to ensure that they promote freedom and recognize others as different from us.[199] When ambiguity is embraced, it shows itself as love and generosity. To treat others with love is to nurture their independence and ensure that the doors of possibility remain open to them. As de Beauvoir writes, "It is only as something strange, forbidden, as something free, that the other is revealed as an other. And to love him genuinely is to love him in his otherness and in that freedom by which he escapes."[200]

For five decades up until his death, de Beauvoir faithfully loved Sartre, her partner and philosophical comrade. They agreed to have an open relationship built on transparency and freedom. At times she would become jealous of Sartre's relationships with others, although she too engaged in love affairs. Both challenged their feelings of jealousy, however, deeming jealousy an enemy of freedom. In 1986, six years after Sartre's death, de Beauvoir was laid to rest in the same tomb as her life-long companion in the Montparnasse cemetery.

# APPLYING DE BEAUVOIR'S PHILOSOPHY

De Beauvoir wants you to understand your freedom as integrally bound up with the freedom of others. Freedom does not mean doing or getting what you want when you want it. Freedom lies in your ability to transcend your given state toward an open horizon of possibilities. You cannot act in a world full of opportunity if others are closing the world off for you; nor can you see possibility in a world devoid of them. If you want to live freely, you must ensure that others can also live freely because these others set the conditions for your freedom. Your actions decide whether the world promotes freedom or denies it. This is how freedom works as an ethical principle. Love is how you let others be in their freedom and difference.

De Beauvoir asks you to acknowledge that the world is ambiguous. Embracing ambiguity is to recognize the potential and promise all around you. Fearing ambiguity is to close off the future by hiding behind ready-made ideas of who you are supposed to be; it is to imprison people behind ideas of who you think they are. Acknowledge others in their difference and their freedom. Free yourself from prejudices and expectations that lead you to limit the world and how you see and approach others. Don't close off your options by entrenching yourself in an identity, or limiting yourself by fixating on a singular goal. You may think that it's easier to have everything figured out by adhering to clearly defined blueprints. Enduring ambiguity may be frightening because it opens you up to the unknown. Instead of fearing uncertainty and ambiguity, see it as the doorway to unimagined possibilities opened up by others. Allow others to introduce you to new worlds. Freedom becomes an ethic when you refrain from controlling others, and instead direct your actions toward creating a space where the other can show themselves to you in their truth.

# QUESTIONS FOR CONSIDERATION

- *Can you think of your freedom as an ethic that is integrally bound up with the freedom of others?*

- *When have you allowed yourself to engage with the world and others in complete openness without expectations or prejudices?*

- *How do you approach the world and others through perspectives that limit how you see and act in the world?*

- *Do you limit the world by seeing it in terms of goals you want to accomplish?*

- *Can you identify situations that prevent others from transcending their present conditions by closing off their futures?*

- *When have you acted to shut down possibilities and close off the future for yourself or others out of fear of the unknown?*

- *Have you ever taken part in actions that help to free people from forms of oppression?*

- *Are you willing to give up your advantages to allow others to live in liberty?*

- *How do you act in ways that demonstrate a fear of uncertainty and of the unknown?*

- *How would you act differently toward others if you viewed them in their difference—an unknown to you?*

- *Are you able to love unconditionally from the perspective of ethical freedom and allow others to be in their difference?*

# Albert Camus

1913 ALGERIA    1960 FRANCE

## *Live Without Appeal to Anything but the Sheer Passion of Life Itself*

Albert Camus is a philosopher of the absurd. He asks us to live without appealing to anything but the sheer joy of life itself. For Camus, life is a flame that needs to be harnessed and lived to the fullest. Making the most of life here and now is Camus's remedy for an existence that has no inherent meaning or certainty, but is simply "absurd." Camus paints a stark picture of the universe. Our lives have no essential purpose, and the world is ultimately indifferent to human existence. At any moment, and without warning or consent, we will be torn from our projects and from our loved ones. The only certainty is that of an untimely death. "It is essential to die unreconciled and not of one's own free will."[201] This is why Camus describes existence as absurd. Nevertheless, we must live joyously "in spite of" this absurdity. Like a condemned inmate savoring their last meal and soaking up the rays of the sun as they take their final steps, Camus asks us to squeeze every drop out of life up until the bitter end. Revolting against the absurd senselessness of existence, we live in "that unbelievable disinterestedness with regard to everything except for the pure flame of life."[202]

Camus's concept of the absurd captures the conflict between our longing for order and reason, and a world that promises nothing. We want meaning, security, and stability, but the world is indifferent to our desires. "The world evades us because it becomes itself again."[203] We desire to make the world familiar and to feel at home—but we are ultimately homeless. An unforeseen event, a tragic loss, an unwelcome illness, or an accident could all awaken us to the futility of our planning and the absurdity of existence. When the meaning of our lives unravels and we stand before a void, we meet the absurd. Camus explains: "This divorce between man and his life, the actor and his setting, is properly the feeling of absurdity."[204] We often encounter the absurd in instants when we see through the charades and mechanical gestures that we, or others, employ just to survive. For Camus, we live in exile, as strangers in the world, and often even as strangers to ourselves. "Just one thing: that denseness and that strangeness of the world is the absurd."[205]

Camus believes that God, the afterlife, and even scientific truths are simply metaphysical comforts we create to feel secure. We live as though we can count on something: the future, our efforts, our planning. But it is an illusion to think that we can direct anything with certainty. Unexpected events beyond our control may alter the course of our lives forever, leaving us scrambling to try and make sense of the senseless. When life gets derailed and thrown off the tracks we have spent our lives laying down, we meet the absurd. It is here, where we experience the randomness of life, that we must rebel. We must take hold of our lives and find happiness in spite of the absurd. "Likewise, and during every day of an illustrious life, time carries us. But a moment always comes when we have to carry it."[206]

Camus is not the first thinker to declare that there is no inherent meaning to existence. But he claims to be the first to live out its consequences. He does not invoke any notion of salvation, or call us to give meaning to our lives. Instead of expecting us to seek meaning, he asks us to act in defiance against the meaninglessness of existence. We do this in what Camus calls "revolt," by finding happiness and experiencing as much as we can. For Camus, judging whether life is worth living answers the fundamental question of philosophy. If we choose life, then we must be defiant against death and passionate about life by living every moment to the maximum. This is how we revolt against the senseless and transitory nature of life. As Camus writes, "The absurd man can only drain everything to the bitter end, and deplete himself."[207] By accepting and embracing the absurd in revolt, we consume everything life has to offer us in the here and now—this is Camus's formula for happiness. "Being aware of one's life, one's revolt, one's freedom, and to the maximum, is living, and to the maximum."[208] To go on living in spite of our losses and pains, even more, to find joy—this is what Camus characterizes as the revolt against the absurd.

Camus wants to free our lives from the boundaries we place around our existence. Chief among these constraints is the concentration of our lives around a set plan. He has little patience for what he calls the "bureaucrats of the mind and heart." These bureaucrats imprison their lives within the walls of a blueprint; they delude themselves that they can control their destinies and fit the world into a box of their design. Stringent plans place limits on our freedom and passions. Instead of opening ourselves to the vastness of possible experiences found in the world, we can see only through the prisms of our expectations. Camus explains: "To the extent to which he imagined a purpose to his life, he adapted himself to the demands of a purpose to be achieved and became the slave of his liberty."[209] Weighing, defining, measuring, and analyzing our lives provides us with a false sense of purpose and security. Such practices rob existence of its vigor. They fail to acknowledge the role of random luck and chance. When we stop trying to control our lives and recognize that much in life is beyond our control, we are prepared to welcome the unexpected. "For the absurd man it is not a matter of explaining and solving, but of experiencing and describing. Everything begins with lucid indifference."[210]

Camus presents his model of the absurd hero through a reinterpretation of the life of the mythical character, Sisyphus. Camus describes Sisyphus as happy in spite of the meaninglessness of his existence. In the myth, we meet Sisyphus after his death. He asks Hades, god of the underworld, to allow him to return to earth so that he can chastise his wife for placing his corpse in the public square and thus failing to abide by tradition. Hades agrees, provided Sisyphus returns quickly. But finding himself under the warmth of the sun before the crashing sounds of the sea and the salt of the air, Sisyphus defies Hades. Passionate about life, he seeks to remain on earth. Eventually, Sisyphus is forced back to the underworld. The gods impose what they think is the most severe sentence any human could endure: the "unspeakable penalty in which the whole being is exerted toward accomplishing nothing."[211] Sisyphus is condemned to ceaselessly roll a rock up a hill, only to watch it fall back down, *ad infinitum*. What Camus finds tragic about Sisyphus is that he is aware of his fate—endless toil stripped of all meaning and purpose. But Camus believes that Sisyphus' fate is not unlike that of the everyday working-class hero, who also toils tirelessly day after day at the same task, saving for a retirement that may never come.

While the story of Sisyphus originally ends with his punishment, Camus imagines more. Defiant against death and passionate about life, Camus imagines Sisyphus as happy. He takes control of his fate the moment he ceases trying to accomplish any particular goal. No longer expecting anything and not having his actions bound to any purpose, Sisyphus is free to enjoy his life.

Camus writes: "There is no fate that cannot be surmounted by scorn."[212] At times the rock is victorious and Sisyphus is melancholy. At other times, he finds joy in spite of the absurd—"he is stronger than his rock."[213] For Camus, detachment and passion crown the splendor and futility of our absurd existence.

We live as if we can count on something: God, science, the future, our efforts, retirement. But tomorrow comes and it may be disappointing. Camus cautions us that every bone in our bodies should be wary of delaying our joy until tomorrow. The only certainty we have is today. Describing those who lack an understanding of the absurd, Camus writes, "He weighs his chances, he counts on 'someday,' his retirement or the labor of his sons. He still thinks that something in his life can be directed."[214] In fact, Camus knew firsthand the absurdity of existence. As a youth in Algeria he showed signs of a promising career in football. He played for the Algerian national team and the Racing Universitaire d'Alger, until this future was halted by tuberculosis. Camus then turned to philosophy and writing. He was the second youngest and first African-born recipient of the Nobel Prize in Literature.

Camus met with the senselessness of the absurd again later in life, his future cut off once and for all by a car accident. Legend has it that Camus, who disliked cars, thought that the most absurd way to die would be in a car crash. The day he died, he was scheduled to take a train back to Paris with his family from his residence in Provence, where he had been writing. But at the last minute his friend and publicist offered him a ride back to Paris in a rare French sports car, a Facel Vega. At the age of 46, Camus died in a car crash on that fatal drive back to Paris. His train ticket was found in his pocket.

In his "Tribute to Camus," Sartre underscores the force of Camus' notion of the absurd: "The particular scandal of his death is the abolition of the human order by the inhuman."[215] Indeed, Camus teaches us that we are born under a universal death sentence from which there is no escape. Life bereaves us of any future security or peace. But for Camus, it is in the simultaneity of the awareness of the absurdity of existence and our revolt against the absurd that we can give value, rather than meaning, to life. "But what does life mean in such a universe?" Camus asks. His response: "Nothing else for the moment but indifference to the future and a desire to use up everything that is given."[216]

# APPLYING CAMUS' PHILOSOPHY

Camus wants you to live your life with gusto and squeeze every moment of joy out of your existence. Do what makes you happy and enjoy what you are doing. Love the process as much as the finished product: the process may be all you get. Death comes without warning. You may never realize your plans or arrive at your destination. At any moment you may be taken away from everything and everyone you love. This is why Camus describes existence as absurd and asks you to live without appealing to anything but the sheer passion of life itself. Live the canvas that is your life and paint it in broad strokes. Give the void its colors. Don't be a bureaucrat of life by waiting for this or that plan to unfold before you start enjoying your life. The absurdity of existence guarantees that the world will not conform to your plans or desires. By hoping and planning you rob yourself of the only moment you have to enjoy life—the present.

Set goals but make sure you enjoy the journey. When things fall apart, chalk it up to the absurd and grab even more tightly to the daily pleasures of living. There is no rhyme or reason to your suffering. The universe is not against you because the universe is not concerned with you. The world owes you nothing. Life is often a matter of chance. Don't spend your time searching for an underlying meaning, or you will lose sight of what is most important—the simple and glorious fact that you are alive now. Find joy in your everyday existence. There is nothing more powerful or joyful than the fact that you are here now; everything else is uncertain and must be met in the indifference of an awareness of the absurd. By constantly holding the absurd in view, you will be reminded to make the best out of every situation and drain every moment to its bitter end. In spite of the absurdity of existence, you can win happiness.

# QUESTIONS FOR CONSIDERATION

- *Do you think it is possible to live a passionate life unhinged from a desire for meaning or purpose?*

- *Can you still find joy when everything seems to have fallen apart?*

- *Are you able to ascribe personal tragedies and troubles to the absurd and see them as random events without any deeper meaning?*

- *Do you make the most of every moment, or are you reserving your happiness for some future time?*

- *Do you pass over life as it happens around you by focusing on a future life you have yet to create?*

- *Do you see the unscripted aspects of life surrounding you, and can you grasp opportunities as they arise?*

- *Do you fail to live spontaneously by living according to a plan of how your life is supposed to be?*

- *Are you living your life to the maximum, or do you simply go through the motions of living?*

- *Can you live happily in the present without hoping for something better yet to come?*

- *Are you able to revolt against the ultimate defeat, that of death, and live fully in the present?*

# Franz Fanon

1925 MARTINIQUE   1961 USA

## *Resistance is World Making*

Franz Fanon is a philosopher of resistance. He asks us to decolonize our minds by revolting against the cultural forces that form and deform our world and self-image. Growing up under French colonial rule in Martinique, and later fighting with the Arabs against French colonialism in Algeria, Fanon experienced the debilitating effects of racism and colonialism first-hand. As a psychiatrist, he documented how the myths of White supremacy became embodied in his patients' everyday thoughts and practices. Feelings of inferiority, trauma, and even madness are the products of racist and colonial oppression that render the oppressed incomprehensible to themselves. This incomprehensibility, Fanon believes, is the impetus for rebellion. "The end of race prejudice begins with a sudden incomprehension."[217] Lacking the soil from which to understand one's self positively and with dignity, the oppressed must rebel. A de-rooting of the ideas that form the colony of the oppressed mind, together with a violent restructuring of society, is how the oppressed can win their dignity. Fanon does not think it possible to reform a system built on the exploitation and oppression of people of color.

Fanon expanded the field of psychiatry to encompass the impact of political and social forces on the psyche and the body. Colonialism not only occupies the land of the subjected, but their minds and bodies as well. Fanon describes the lived experience of Blackness as an experience of viewing his body in the third person. Finding himself trapped within the color of his skin, he saw himself not as a subject, but as an object of the stories that White people told about him. Fanon describes a simple walk down a city street, and the irony in a child's cry that freezes him in the identity imposed on Black men. "'Mama, see the Negro! I'm frightened!' Frightened! Frightened! Now they were beginning to be afraid of me. I made up my mind to laugh myself to tears, but laughter had become impossible. I could no longer laugh, because I already knew that there were legends, stories, history . . . I was responsible at the same time for my body, for my race, for my ancestors. I subjected myself to an objective examination, I discovered my blackness, my ethnic characteristics; and I was battered down by tom-toms, cannibalism, intellectual deficiency, fetishism, racial defects, slave-ships, and above all else, above all: 'Sho' good eatin.'"[218]

Fanon provides us with the tools to resist colonial and racial oppression and create new spaces of liberation. A pioneer in the fields of post-structural, postcolonial, and cultural studies, Fanon challenges the hierarchical model of power that controls solely through laws, prohibitions, and punishments. He views power as something that is diffused throughout society: it unfolds in institutions and organizes the spaces of culture within which we move and come to understand ourselves. Fanon explains how the reach of colonial power permeates every aspect of existence. It infiltrates how the oppressed view their bodies and carry themselves within the world. The concepts of race, gender, and sexuality work to organize our behavior and station us in relation to others. Whiteness, for example, gains its sense of purity and superiority only in relation to Blackness

*Philosophy Wise*

and other people of color who are deemed inferior and in need of being civilized. This is why Fanon states that "In fact, the settler is right when he speaks of knowing 'them' well. For it is the settler who has brought the native into existence and who perpetuates his existence. The settler owes the fact of his very existence, that is to say, his property, to the colonial system."[219]

For Fanon, there are no universal truths or fixed histories. The world is created by human action; truths are historically given and created by those in power. Reality is therefore plural and relative, always subject to change. Science, too, is a product of our making: there is no such thing as pure objectivity. In the hands of the colonizer, science is used to establish classifications and categories that normalize existing networks of power by fortifying race, gender, class, and sex inequalities. The concepts we use to understand ourselves, how we gain knowledge and what we deem to be knowledge, even the very languages we speak, are all informed by the dominant culture within which we find ourselves. Colonialism leaves nothing untouched. All aspects of culture within colonial systems are informed by anti-Black racism. "All round me the white man, above the sky tears at its navel, the earth rasps under my feet, and there is a white song, a white song. All this whiteness that burns me . . . I sit down at the fire and I become aware of my uniform. I had not seen it. It is indeed ugly."[220]

Fanon asks us to pay attention to how we are made to feel inferior by seeing ourselves through oppressive categories that rob us of our power. Born into the world believing he could attain anything, Fanon eventually found himself crushed by the White world and robbed of his freedom to create a meaningful life. He was expected to act not as a man, but as a Black man in a world made by White people. "I am the slave not of the 'idea' that others have of me but of my own appearance. I move slowly in the world, accustomed now to seek no longer for upheaval. I progress by crawling. And already I am being dissected under white eyes, the only real eyes. I am fixed."[221] He describes being caught in the paradox of non-being, wherein he is made to feel invisible and unworthy. As objects defined in opposition to Whites, he concludes that people of color will never attain equality or justice in a world that negates Blackness. No amount of education or cultural assimilation into Western values will liberate Black people, and Whiteness is the only viable identity in a world built on the oppression of people of color.

Fanon teaches us how to unlock ourselves from oppressive racial and cultural identities. We do this through questioning, reflection, and violent struggle. "O my body, make of me always a man who questions!"[222] He warns against wearing "white masks" and assimilating into the mainstream. Assimilation will never bring the oppressed closer to power and privilege, no matter how hard one tries. Black oppression is built into the mainstream values of White society. By understanding and expressing ourselves in the language and worldviews of those who oppress us, we unwittingly participate in our own alienation and oppression. For Fanon, racism and the debasement of people of color is rooted in irrationalism. It is impossible to engage rationally with the incoherence of White supremacy and other forms of oppression.

> I had rationalized the world and the world had rejected me on the basis of color prejudice. Since no agreement was possible on the level of ireason, I threw myself back toward unreason. It was up to the white man to be more irrational than I. Out of the necessities of my struggle I had chosen the method of regression, but the fact remained that it was an unfamiliar weapon; here I am at home; I am made of the irrational; I wade in the irrational. Up to the neck in the irrational.
> And now how my voice vibrates!

*Philosophy Wise*

Those who invented neither gunpowder nor the compass.
Those who never learned to conquer steam or electricity.
Those who never explored the seas or the skies.
But they know the farthest corners of the land of anguish.
Those who never knew any journey save that of abduction.
Those who learned to kneel in docility.
Those who were domesticated and Christianized.
Those who were injected with bastardy . . .
Yes, all those are my brothers—a "bitter brotherhood"
imprisons all of us alike.[223]

Fanon explains that he had every reason to hate his oppressors. Made to feel insignificant, unworthy, and less than human, he was nevertheless ready to forgive the atrocities of colonial aggression. Yet rather than asking for his forgiveness, his oppressors rejected him. Fanon elaborates: "What? While I was forgetting, forgiving, and wanting only to love, my message was flung back in my face like a slap. The white world, the only honorable one, barred me from all participation. A man was expected to behave like a man. I was expected to behave like a black man—or at least like a [Negro]."[224] As a black man he was forced into the "zone of non-being" and rendered insignificant. Because racism and the myth of White supremacy are not logical, Black people and all colonized people have no alternative but to destroy the entire apparatus of colonial and racist rule.

Fanon wants us not to hope for change, but to see oppressive systems for what they are so that we may actively work to dismantle them. Colonial power is not content with dominating the minds of those whom it oppresses; it also distorts, perverts, and destroys their histories. Colonialism is dependent on the exploitation and extraction of people from their lands and from their past. As Fanon reminds us, "Europe's well-being and progress were built with the sweat and corpses of blacks, Arabs,

Indians, and Asians."[225] Robbed of any sources from which to build a positive sense of self, the oppressed must fight to win anew their dignity and sanity. Coming to see the oppressors for who they truly are, a decolonized mind no longer feels the need to catch up with the West, or imitate its rapacious ways. He writes: "The people come to understand that wealth is not the fruit of labour but the result of organized, protected robbery. Rich people are no longer respectable people; they are nothing more than flesh eating animals, jackals and vultures which wallow in the people's blood."[226]

For Fanon, there is no dignity without the ability to create oneself and move freely in a world of one's own making. Tortured, alienated, depressed, depicted as ignorant and savage, the only alternative left to the oppressed is revolution. The violence of colonialism must be met with violence. The oppressed must destroy the culture, laws, and principles that negate their humanity and then institute a new humanism along with the redistribution of wealth to the poor and dispossessed. For Fanon, violence is world-making: "National liberation, national reawakening, restoration of the nation to the people or Commonwealth, whatever the name used, whatever the latest expression, decolonization is always a violent event."[227]

Fanon asks us to build ourselves up not by turning to sources of strength from our pasts, but by preparing the earth for new possibilities of self-expression in a post-revolutionary world. To end oppression and exploitation, a totally new global re-orientation is needed. The colonial world built by Europeans cannot be reformed—it must be destroyed. Fanon does not describe what a post-revolutionary world would look like, although he does state that it should not seek to revive pre-colonial customs and folklore. Fanon believes that culture stands opposed to custom and tradition. Custom and tradition are static, rather than dynamic and unfolding within history. For Fanon, the past is disposable; it has been lost to the manipulations and distortions of the oppressors. Real creativity therefore cannot come from worn-out customs and traditions. Years of colonial domination have stripped old cultural remnants of their living force. The newly liberated should embrace instead the ambiguity of an unknown future.

Decolonization of the mind requires us to investigate and sweep away the oppressive ideas that have taken root in our minds. The oppressed must tear down colonial models that have ingrained themselves in their consciousness and create new spaces of culture. Again, Fanon does not define what these spaces look like. He believes a new society will arise out of the practices and struggles of revolution. "Decolonization, as we know, is a historical process, that is to say that it cannot be understood, it cannot become intelligible nor clear to itself except in the exact measure that we can discern the movements which give it historical form and content."[228] No longer gripped by the cages of identity constructed by their oppressors, the newly liberated will rise to create a world of their own making. Educated not to repeat the atrocities of their colonizers, and no longer haunted by the spirits of the past, the liberated will be free to create a new humanism that will allow for creative modes of self-understanding and expression. With this new humanism, a new human is in the making, replacing the older forms of humanity: "After the conflict there is not only the disappearance of colonialism but also the disappearance of the colonized man."[229] Fanon asks us to embrace the uncertainty of a new tomorrow as the only possibility for ridding ourselves of an oppressive past.

# APPLYING FANON'S PHILOSOPHY

Fanon wants you to notice how you may be seeing yourself through oppressive categories such as race, gender, and sexuality. Think about how your psyche has been damaged and colonized by internalizing myths about who you are that have been created by those seeking to dominate you. Don't try to gain acceptance by changing yourself to conform to prevailing standards. Trying to assimilate into dominant cultural values will not liberate you if you are relegated to the margins. Your oppression is built into the dominant culture you want to become part of. Take note of how cultural forces shape how you experience yourself and how you understand your place in the world. Pay attention to mechanisms that make you feel insignificant, unworthy, and less than human. Fanon does not think you can rise up within a system that is built on your oppression and subjugation. The only way for the oppressed to own their minds and bodies, and overcome feelings of inferiority and alienation, is to fight for independence.

Decolonize your mind by forming new models for self-understanding. Be part of the movement to destroy the institutions that negate your humanity; work to create new values and new forms of relating to yourself and others. Fanon does not think that going back to your roots will provide you with a basis for self-worth. You are not tied to your past, and your past has likely been debased by those exploiting you. He asks you to build a new society out of your struggles for social justice. Don't be concerned that you don't have a model for what this society or your new self in a free world will look like. Who you are to become once you have thrown off the shackles that bind you will arise from your battles to realize your humanity. Take action to build a world with others who are committed to liberation. If you have been robbed of the space to live with dignity, there is little choice but to fight for your freedom. Sometimes the only way to overcome the violence of colonial rule is through violent struggle.

# QUESTIONS FOR CONSIDERATION

- *Has your psyche been damaged by internalizing other people's oppressive ideas about who you are?*

- *Can you identify how social categories of race, gender, class, and sexuality influence how you see yourself and others?*

- *Are you able to identify how power structures position you in society and in relation to others?*

- *Do you participate in your own self-alienation by wearing masks and buying into the values of a dominant culture that does not respect your difference?*

- *What are the sources for your understanding of beauty, and what standards of beauty do you apply to yourself?*

- *How would you live your life differently outside of cultural categories that imprison your self-understanding and make you feel inferior?*

- *Are you allowing yourself to be colonized in passive ways by seeking the approval of those who are threatened by you and wish to cast you aside?*

- *How may you be participating in the oppression of others by taking advantage of unearned and unacknowledged privileges?*

- *Are there any occasions on which you would fight to address injustice?*

- *How could it be liberating to reinvent yourself without drawing on sources from your past?*

# Gloria Anzaldúa

1942 USA    2004 USA

## *To Survive the Borderlands Be a Crossroads*

Gloria Anzaldúa is a philosopher of *mestiza* consciousness. She asks us to reject the myth of the consistent and uniform self and to embrace the multiplicity of mixed and splintered identities. The *mestiza* is a woman who straddles two or more cultures, languages, or value systems. *Mestizas* are what Anzaldúa calls "threshold" people who do not fit squarely into one fixed identity, way of life, or geographical location. They live at the borderlands, standing at the margins of society while moving within and among different and often conflicting worlds. "From this racial, ideological, cultural, and biological cross pollinization, an alien consciousness is presently in the making—a new *mestiza* consciousness, *una conciencia de mujer*. It is a consciousness of the Borderlands."[230]

Anzaldúa asks us to be aware of the differences that exist between us and those from different cultures. She also asks those who are struggling to find their place within new cultures to be aware of the differences within themselves. Writing primarily

in English, but peppering her discussion of *mestiza* consciousness with Spanish phrases, Anzaldúa puts her non-Spanish
readers into an uncomfortable outsider position. This parallels
the discomfort felt by many immigrants when they are confronted with a language they don't understand. In this way,
Anzaldúa describes and invokes an appreciation of the inner
conflict experienced by those straddling cultures, languages,
or value systems. She resists the exclusionary practices of a
culture that demands a uniform identity. This demand stems
from the dominant culture's (in her case, White culture's)
desperate need for boundary lines, and desire for purity. She
asks us not to internalize the dominant culture or its call for
purity, but to embrace the ambiguity of mixed identities and
to live at the crossroads. "To survive the Borderlands/ you
must live *sin fronteras*/ be a crossroads." Anzaldúa also uses
the term *nepantleras*. This term is adopted from an Aztec concept meaning "torn between ways," and she uses it to describe
the *mestiza* consciousness of those who live in the threshold
of the "in-between." "*Nepantleras* are threshold people: they
move within and among multiple, often conflicting, worlds and
refuse to align themselves exclusively with any single individual,
group, or belief system."[231]

As a Chicana woman born in south Texas, with layered cultural
and social allegiances, Anzaldúa refuses to be split by labels.
Acknowledging the difficulties involved in refusing to identify
with any one identity, she asks *mestizas* to open themselves to
personal risks and potential wounds. These wounds include
self-division, isolation, misunderstanding, rejection, and ac-
cusations of disloyalty. Here, Anzaldúa characterizes her fight
to juggle her multiple identities and her resistance to conform to
the expectations imposed upon her to choose a side. "I am a
wind-swayed bridge, a crossroads inhabited by whirlwinds.
Gloria, the facilitator, Gloria the mediator, straddling the walls
between abysses. 'Your allegiance is to *La Raza*, the Chicano

movement,' say the members of my race. 'Your allegiance is to the Third World,' say my Black and Asian friends. 'Your allegiance is to your gender, to women,' say the feminists. Then there's my allegiance to the Gay movement, to the socialist revolution, to the New Age, to magic and the occult. And there's my affinity to literature, to the world of the artist. What am I? *A third world lesbian feminist with Marxist and mystic leanings.* They would chop me up into little fragments and tag each piece with a label . . . Who, me confused? Ambivalent? Not so. Only your labels split me."[232]

Anzaldúa empowers us to live in transitional spaces and to shift between multiple identities. Having to negotiate her Mexican, Indigenous, and American identities, often in conflict with each other, she describes being torn in an inner struggle. A special kind of strength is required to combat the psychic restlessness of those who find themselves living in states of perpetual transition. Confusion and anxiety are often unavoidable consequences of accepting a fractured identity. She explains that "The ambivalence from the clash of voices results in mental and emotional states of perplexity. Internal strife results in insecurity and indecisiveness. The *mestiza's* dual or multiple personality is plagued by psychic restlessness."[233]

To deal with the isolation and loneliness of being at the borderlands, Anzaldúa creates a sanctuary that she calls *el mundo zurdo* (the left-handed world). In this visionary place, she can travel in and out of different worlds as she pleases. Occupying the liminal space between different cultures and worlds, she imagines herself to be like the Hindu god Shiva: "a many-armed and legged body with one foot on brown soil, one on white, one in straight society, one in the gay world, the man's world, the women's, one limb in the literary world, another in the working class, the socialist, and the occult worlds."[234] Anzaldúa's vision of *el mundo zurdo* presents us with a vivid understanding of how to expand our horizons and lifestyles. She shows us how we may escape the confines that point us aggressively toward a unitary state of existence formed around a single identity.

Anzaldúa warns us against occupying any one stance. She asks us to reject cultural expectations about who we are supposed to be, and how we are supposed to live. Participating in different and diverse worlds, rather than identifying solely with one group or identity, Anzaldúa explodes the borders of identities that build walls between people. For her, restlessness and homelessness make inclusion and difference possible. Understanding that no culture is monolithic, *mestizas* can use their movements among divergent worlds to develop innovative, potentially transformative, perspectives and lifestyles. "She is willing to share, to make herself vulnerable to foreign ways of seeing and thinking. She surrenders all notions of safety, of the familiar. Deconstruct, construct. She becomes a *nahual*, able to transform herself into a tree, a coyote, into another person. She learns to transform the small 'I' into the total Self. *Se hace moldeadora de su alma. Según la concepción que tiene de sí misma, así será.*"[235]

Threshold people welcome differences within and among diverse groups to make room for new forms of community and new types of social action. At first, the marginalized may have to take an active stand against the dominant culture. Those of mixed border identities will likely find themselves challenging patriarchal, dominant, or majority-held cultural norms. But they must not stop at this challenge or take up an oppositional identity. Opposition keeps in place the binary of oppressed and oppressor and leaves fixed the common denominator of violence. "All reaction is limited by, and dependent on, what it is reacting against."[236] An acute awareness is needed of the manifold and fluid principles that govern traveling between identities.

Anzaldúa describes being haunted by the racism and sexism that she internalized and practiced when she was younger. She had darker skin, but was taught to think that white skin was beautiful and dark skin worthless. As a lesbian growing up in a patriarchal Latino culture, Anzaldúa also observed conditions that promoted female subservience and deference to male authority and heterosexual norms. Women were expected to understand themselves narrowly within the framework of mother and wife. Anzaldúa points out that omnipresent social categories such as race, gender, and sexuality limit individual creativity. They condition how women and people of color see themselves and others. She calls upon men to join the feminist struggle and admit the harm they have caused women and themselves by taking up a patriarchal identity.

Seeing the world from different perspectives, the mestiza creates a new consciousness that rises above separations and dualities. Anzaldúa invites whites to join in the struggle for liberation. If they are to be comrades, however, whites must first acknowledge their rejection of difference and the ways they have robbed people of color of their land, dignity, and selfhood. "We need you to make public restitution: to say that, to compensate for your own sense of defectiveness, you strive for power over us, you erase our history and our experience because it makes you feel guilty—you'd rather forget your brutish acts."[237]

For Anzaldúa, change happens on the individual level before it rises to the societal level. "Nothing happens in the 'real' world," she writes, "unless it first happens in the images in our heads."[238] White people must learn about the ways in which they dominate and oppress people of color. People of color must learn about their own histories and the histories of their oppression. Anzaldúa calls upon Mexicans specifically to acknowledge their own racism and to welcome their indigenous lineage. An understanding of dual existence and the perspectives that go with it is essential. Adopting a new consciousness of the borderlands is an evolutionary process of growth.

Anzaldúa asks us to be flexible and to avoid the desire to cling to a fixed identity. Having no fixed home or culture may be unsettling, but it is also a gateway that allows for openness and participation in all cultures and identity groups. Enduring the discomfort of standing at different shorelines is a prerequisite for personal transformation and social and political change. By remaining flexible we can discard the Western reliance on rational analysis: a reliance that drives us toward fixed goals and set patterns. Anzaldúa asks those at the threshold to embrace ambiguity as a way of life that strives toward inclusion and diversity. "She learns to be an Indian in Mexican culture, to be Mexican from an Anglo point of view. She learns to juggle cultures. She has a plural personality, she operates in a pluralistic mode—nothing is thrust out, the good, the bad, and the ugly, nothing rejected, nothing abandoned. Not only does she sustain contradictions, she turns the ambivalence into something else."[239]

Freeing ourselves from any fixed perspective allows us to welcome difference and join with others as citizens of the universe. Yet lacking a firm footing in one soil is physically, emotionally, and psychically destabilizing. Living at the crossroads amidst cultural collisions is unhinging because it is unstable and there are no roadmaps guiding the future. Anzaldúa encourages us to keep going: *"Caminante, no hay puentes, se hace puentes al andar* [Voyager, there are no bridges, one builds them as one walks]."[240] To be ambivalent in the multiple worlds one inhabits is to endure the pain of continual upheaval and change. This is why Anzaldúa relies on spirituality to support her during the moments when she questions her own sanity.

"I am mad—but I chose this madness."[241] Renewal and change is the way of the *mestiza*. Like those caring for the earth as they plant and tend to the soil, she asks us to follow nature's rhythms of growth, decay, death, and birth. Embracing and reinventing ambivalence by turning it into an opportunity to welcome difference is Anzaldúa's innovative and evolutionary message to us.

# APPLYING ANZALDÚA'S PHILOSOPHY

Anzaldúa wants you to embrace the multiplicity of mixed and splintered identities. If you are a person straddling two or more cultures, languages, or value systems, then she encourages you to adopt a *mestiza,* or borderland consciousness. Release yourself from the myth of purity. Resist the demand to speak as a unified and uniform self. Welcome and experiment with all the different elements that make up who you are, and find new ways to express yourself. Don't allow yourself to be split by labels. It is time for you to escape cultural expectations about who you are supposed to be. As a *mestiza,* you can exist at the threshold and travel within and among different worlds.

Broaden your horizons by standing in the cracks between borders. Gain a wider understanding of yourself and others and awaken to new ways of living in the world at the threshold of liminal spaces. Transformation is born out of living in the in-between. As you begin to see from multiple perspectives, you will no longer accept the superiority of any one culture, race, sex, or identity. Embrace a new mythos and form new communities that respect no boundaries. You do not need to plant your feet in any one soil. Find comfort in occupying transitional spaces. Initially, you may feel moments of anxiety, isolation and loneliness by refusing to identify with any one culture. Remember, you are strong enough to endure the ambiguity and contradictions of a flexible identity that will allow you to enter into many different worlds. Resist the call to belong to a defined group, even if you get called disloyal as a result. Allow yourself to shift between the various identities and value structures that make up who you are. There is no single correct way to see or to be in the world.

# QUESTIONS FOR CONSIDERATION

- *What are the different identities and allegiances that make up your self-understanding?*

- *Do you feel divided by being mixed race or by belonging to different cultures that may be in conflict with each other?*

- *Do you experience confusion and anxiety because you do not fit into one identity box?*

- *Do you abandon parts of yourself so that you can more easily identify with one social or cultural group?*

- *How would you be transformed by giving space to and moving freely between the different cultural aspects that shape you?*

- *Can you straddle different worlds and shift between different perspectives? What does this feel like?*

- *Do you choose how you want to identify, or have you adopted your identity categories from your culture, family, or other sources?*

- *Are you worried about being called a traitor by refusing to identify completely with any one group?*

- *Can you imagine how refusing to identify with any one racial group could weaken the boundaries of fixed racial divisions?*

*Gloria Anzaldúa*

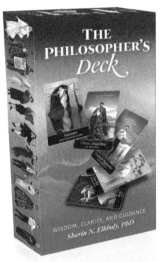

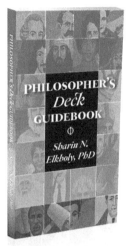

Simone de Beauvoir

ETHICAL FREEDOM

PLAYING WITH
## *The Philosopher's Deck*

Now that you have begun your journey with these thinkers, you may want to deepen your intuitions through hands on engagement with *The Philosopher's Deck*. *The Philosopher's Deck* and accompanying *Guidebook* are companion pieces to *Philosophy Wise*. Use the deck to open up pathways for reflection, introspection, practice, and self-understanding. Gain inspiration and the clarity of good thinking by drawing on the wisdom of the greats and see what the cards have in store for you.

philosophywise.com

# ENDNOTES

*(Use the resources in the Endnotes to further explore each Philosopher's original works)*

## Socrates

1   Plato, *Crito*, Translator, Benjamin Jowett, The Internet Classics Archive / MIT. (Crito—sec. 48b).   http://classics.mit.edu/Plato/crito.html

2   Nietzsche, Friedrich, *The Portable Nietzsche* (p. 472, *Twilight of the Idols*—sec. 5 The Problem of Socrates) / translated by Walter Kaufmann. London: Penguin Books *Viking Portable*, 1954.   https://archive.org/details/ThePortableNietzscheWalterKaufmann/page/n487/mode/2up

3   Ibid.   http://classics.mit.edu/Plato/apology.html (*Apology*—30b).

4   Ibid.   http://classics.mit.edu/Plato/apology.html (*Apology*—30b).

5   Ibid.   http://classics.mit.edu/Plato/apology.html (*Apology*—sec. 21d).

6   Ibid.   http://classics.mit.edu/Plato/apology.html

7   Ibid.   http://classics.mit.edu/Plato/apology.html

8   Ibid.   http://classics.mit.edu/Plato/apology.html (*Apology*—sec. 30e)

9   Plato, *The Republic*, Translator, Benjamin Jowett, ( *Republic*—516 a-e).   http://classics.mit.edu/Plato/republic.html

10   Plato, *The Apology*, Translator, Benjamin Jowett, The Internet Classics Archive / MIT.edu   http://classics.mit.edu/Plato/apology.html

11   Ibid.   http://classics.mit.edu/Plato/apology.html

## Lao Tzu

12   Lao-Tzu, Tao Te Ching, Translated by James Legge, The Internet Classics Archive, MIT.edu   http://classics.mit.edu/Lao/taote.html (Chapter 25).

13   Ibid. (chapter 64, see also 17,23)

14   Ibid. (chapter 48)

15   Ibid. (chapter 4)

16   Ibid. (chapter 11)

17   Ibid. (chapter 37)

18   Ibid. (chapter 15)

19   Ibid. (chapter 3)

20   Ibid. (chapter 43)

21   Ibid. (chapter 16)

22   Watson, Burton Translator, *Zhuzngzi—Basic Writings* (p.141). New York: Columbia University Press, 2003.   https://archive.org/details/zhuangzibasicwri00zhua/page/141/mode/2up

23 Cranmer-Byng, L. & Kapadia, Dr. S.A. Editors, *The Buddha's "Way of Virtue"* / translated by W.D.C. Wagiswara & K.J. Saunders. New York: EP Dutton & Co. 1912. https://archive.org/details/buddhaswayofvirt00newyiala/page/52/mode/2up

24 Rāhula, Walpola *What The Buddha Taught*. New York: Grove Press 1959. https://archive.org/details/whatbuddhataught00walp/page/24/mode/2up

25 Ibid. https://archive.org/details/whatbuddhataught00walp/page/10/mode/2up

26 Faswaran, Eknoth: *The Dhammapada* (Classics of Indian Spirituality) (p.206). Canada: Nilgiri Press, 2007.

27 Rāhula, Walpola *What The Buddha Taught*. New York: Grove Press 1959. https://archive.org/details/whatbuddhataught00walp/page/26/mode/2up

28 Cranmer-Byng, L. & Kapadia, Dr. S.A. Editors, *The Buddha's "Way of Virtue"A Translation of the Dhammapada*/ translated by W.D.C. Wagiswara & K.J. Saunders. New York: EP Dutton & Co. 1912. https://archive.org/details/buddhaswayofvirt00newyiala/page/83/mode/2up

29 Young-Eisendrath, Polly *The Gifts of Suffering: Finding Insight, Compassion, and Reward*. Reading, Mass.: Addison-Wesley, Publishing Co., 1996, (259 pages. Pg 150).

30 Cranmer-Byng, L. & Kapadia, Dr. S.A. Editors, *The Buddha's "Way of Virtue" A Translation of the Dhammapada* / translated by W.D.C. Wagiswara & K.J. Saunders. New York: EP Dutton & Co. 1912. https://archive.org/details/buddhaswayofvirt00newyiala/page/64/mode/2up

31 https://archive.org/details/buddhaswayofvirt00newyiala/page/26/mode/2up

32 Ibid. https://archive.org/details/buddhaswayofvirt00newyiala/page/25/mode/2up

33 Ibid. https://archive.org/details/buddhaswayofvirt00newyiala/page/32/mode/2up

34 Ibid. https://archive.org/details/buddhaswayofvirt00newyiala/page/38/mode/2up

35 Faswaran, Eknoth The Dhammapada (Classics of Indian Spirituality) (p.46). Canada: Nilgiri Press, 2007.

36 Rāhula, Walpola *What The Buddha Taught*. New York: Grove Press 1959. https://archive.org/details/whatbuddhataught00walp/page/1112/mode/2up

## Confucius

37 Confucius, [*The analects*] ([6:27]) Translated by Cai, Jack. Madison, WI: Americd-rom Publ. Co 1988. https://archive.org/details/readingsinclassi-00chat/page/18/mode/2up

38 Ibid. ([4:23]) https://archive.org/details/analectsofconfuc00conf_1/page/38/mode/2up

39 Ibid. ([20:3]) https://archive.org/details/analectsofconfuc00conf_1/page/188/mode/2up

40 Ibid. ([15:30]). https://archive.org/details/analectsofconfuc00conf_1/page/188/mode/2up

41 Ibid. ([14:23]) https://archive.org/details/analectsofconfuc00conf_1/page/166/mode/2up

42 Ibid. ([7:27]) https://archive.org/details/analectsofconfuc00conf_1/page/166/mode/2up

43 Ibid. ([9:13]) https://archive.org/details/analectsofconfuc00conf_1/page/94/mode/2up:

44 Ibid. ([4:16]) https://archive.org/details/analectsofconfuc00conf_1/page/36/mode/2up

45 Ibid. ([15:23]) https://archive.org/details/analectsofconfuc00conf_1/page/36/mode/2up

46 Ibid. ([17:2]) https://archive.org/details/readingsinclassi00chat/page/204/mode/2up

47 Ibid. ([1:1]) https://archive.org/details/readingsinclassi00chat/page/204/mode/2up

48 Ibid. ([15:18]) https://archive.org/details/readingsinclassi00chat/page/40/mode/2up

49 Ibid. ([12:11]) https://archive.org/details/analectsofconfuc00conf_1/page/136/mode/2up:

## Aristotle

50 Aristotle, *The Nicomachean Ethics*, translated by Thompson, J.A.K. Baltimore, MD: Penguin Books, 1959. https://archive.org/details/ethicsofaristotl00aris/page/41/mode/2up

51 Ibid. (p.41. 1098:20) https://archive.org/details/ethicsofaristotl00aris/page/41/mode/2up

52 Ibid. (p.73) https://archive.org/details/ethicsofaristotl00aris/page/73/mode/2up

53 Ibid. (p.59) https://archive.org/details/ethicsofaristotl00aris/page/59/mode/2up

54 Ibid. (p.89) https://archive.org/details/ethicsofaristotl00aris/page/89/mode/2up

55   Ibid. (p.284)   https://archive.org/details/ethicsofaristotl00aris/page/284/mode/2up

56   Ibid. (p.284)   https://archive.org/details/ethicsofaristotl00aris/page/284/mode/2up

57   Ibid (p.273)   https://archive.org/details/ethicsofaristotl00aris/page/273/mode/2up

58   Ibid. (p.257)   https://archive.org/details/moraldiscoursese00epicuoft/page/257/mode/2up

### Epictetus

59   Epictetus ,*The Enchiridion* [section 1] (translated by Elizabeth Carter). *The Internet Classics Archive,* MIT.edu, http://classics.mit.edu/Epictetus/epicench.html

60   Ibid. [section 28]

61   Ibid. [section 38]

62   Ibid. [section 8]

63   Ibid. [section 14]

64   Ibid. [section 26]

65   Ibid. (section 11)

66   Ibid. [chapter 11]

67   Aurelius, *The Meditations* (p.68). Chicago: Gateway Editions, 1956. https://archive.org/details/meditationsofmar0000aure/page/68/mode/2up

68   Epictetus *The Enchiridion* [chapter 43] (translated by Elizabeth Carter). MIT online, *The Internet Classics Archive*: http://classics.mit.edu/Epictetus/epicench.html

69   Aurelius *The Meditations* (p.68). Chicago: Gateway Editions, 1956. https://archive.org/details/meditationsofmar0000aure/page/68/mode/2up

70   "Serenity Prayer", Attributed author Niebuhr, Reinhold, Theologian 1932. https://www.prayerfoundation.org/dailyoffice/serenity_prayer_full_version.htm

### Augustine

71   Augustine of Hippo *The Confessions of St. Augustine*. Boston: E.P. Peabody, 1842. https://archive.org/details/cu31924029217309/page/n265/mode/2up

72   credeutintelligas Tract. Ev. Jo., 29.6

73   Augustine of Hippo *The Confessions of St. Augustine*. Boston: E.P. Peabody, 1842. https://archive.org/details/cu31924029217309/page/n265/mode/2up

74   Ibid. https://archive.org/details/cu31924029217309/page/n121/mode/2up

75   Ibid. https://archive.org/details/cu31924029217309/page/n35/mode/2up

76    Ibid.    https://archive.org/details/cu31924029217309/page/n199/mode/2up

77    Ibid.    https://archive.org/details/cu31924029217309/page/n207/mode/2up

78    Ibid.    https://archive.org/details/cu31924029217309/page/n17/mode/2up

79    Ibid.    https://archive.org/details/cu31924029217309/page/n147/mode/2up

### Rumi

80    Schimmel, Annemarie *A Two Colored Brocade* (p.250). North Carolina: University of North Carolina Press, 1997.    https://books.google.com/books?id=JFxO-AgAAQBAJ&pg=PA250&lpg=PA250&dq

81    "The Guest House." WHINFIELD, E.H. Translator *Teachings of Rumi—The Mansavi*. New York: EP Dutton & Co., Inc. 1975.    https://archive.org/details/teachingsofrumithemasnavi/page/n3/mode

82    Barks, Coleman w/ Moyne, J. *The Essential Rumi* (p.48). San Francisco: Harper, 1995.    https://archive.org/details/essentialrumi00jala/page/n7/mode/2up

83    "In your Light." Ibid.

84    *Rumi The Sufi Path of Love* (p.308). Albany: State of New York University Press, 1983.    https://archive.org/details/sufipathoflovesp0000jall/page/308/mode/2up

85    Barks, Coleman, Translator, *Rumi: The Book of Love (*p.163*).* New York: Harper Collins eBooks.    https://archive.org/detailsw/colemanbarksrumithebooko-flovepoemsofecstasyandlongingharperone2005/page/n163/mode/2up

86    *Rumi The Sufi Path of Love* (p.218). Albany: State of New York University Press, 1983.    https://archive.org/details/sufipathoflovesp0000jall/page/218/mode/2up

87    Barks, Coleman, Translator, *The Illuminated Rumi* (p.86). New York: Broadway Books, 1997.

88    Whinfield, E.H. Translator *Teachings of Rumi—The Mansavi*. New York: EP Dutton & Co., Inc. 1975.    https://archive.org/details/teachingsofrumithe-masnavi/page/n3/mode

89    Chittick, William, Translator, The Sufi Path of Love, The Spiritual Teachings of Rumi (p.319). New York: State University of New York Press, 1983:    https://archive.org/details/TheSufiPathOfLoveWilliamC.Chittick/page/319/mode/2up

90    "The Circle and the Zero," WHINFIELD, E.H. Translator *Teachings of Rumi—The Mansavi*. New York: EP Dutton & Co., Inc. 1975.    https://archive.org/details/teachingsofrumithemasnavi/page/n3/mode

91    "A Great Wagon." Ibid (p.147). "Out beyond ideas of wrongdoing and right doing there is a field. I'll meet you there. When the soul lies down in that grass, the world is too full to talk about. Ideas, language, even the phrase each other, doesn't make any sense. The breeze at dawn has secrets to tell you. Don't go back to sleep. You must ask for what you really want. Don't go back to sleep. People are going back and forth across the doorsill where the two worlds

touch. The door is round and open. Don't go back to sleep." https://archive. org/details/colemanbarksrumithebookoflovepoemsofecstasyandlongingharp- erone2005/page/n171/mode/2up

92  Ibid (p. 11). Poems from the Divan-I Shams-I Tabriz, c. 1270 C

93  Whinfield, E.H. Translator *Teachings of Rumi—The Mansavi*. New York: EP Dutton & Co., Inc. 1975.  https://archive.org/details/teachingsofrumithe- masnavi/page/n3/mode

94  Barks, Coleman, *Rumi: The Book of Love Poems and Ecstasy and Longing* (p.66). New York: HarperOne, 2005.  https://archive.org/details/coleman- barksrumithebookoflovepoemsofecstasyandlonginharperone2005/page/ n91/mode/2up

95  Van de Weyer, Robert—editor *Rumi In A Nutshell* (p.29). London: Hodder & Stoughton, 1998.  https://archive.org/details/rumi0000jala/page/29/ mode/2up

96  Ibid. (p.29)

97  Barks, Coleman *Rumi: The Book of Love (*p.33*).* New York: Harper Collins eBooks.  https://archive.org/details/colemanbarksrumithebookoflovepoem- sofecstasyandlonginharperone2005/page/n57/mode/2up

98  Barks, Coleman Translator :*Rumi The Big Red Book* (p.28). New York: Harper- One, 2010.  https://archive.org/details/rumibigredbookgr0000jall/page/28/ mode/2up

99  Chittick, William The Sufi Path of Love, The Spiritual Teachings of Rumi (p.226). New York: State University of New York Press, 1983:  https://archive. org/details/sufipathoflovesp0000jall/page/226/mode/2up

100  Barks, Coleman Translator :*Rumi The Big Red Book* (p.272). New York: HarperOne, 2010.  https://archive.org/details/rumibigredbookgr0000jall/ page/272/mode/2up

### Descartes

101  Cottingham, John Ed. *The Cambridge Companion to Descartes*. UK: Cambridge University Press 1992.

102  Descartes, Rene, *Meditations on First Philosophy* (1639) / Translated by John Cottingham (Second Meditation)  https://www.marxists.org/reference/archive/ descartes/1639/meditations.htm

103  Descartes, Rene, *Discourse on Method* / Translator: John Veitch. Project Guten- berg online  https://www.gutenberg.org/files/59/59-h/59-h.htm (Book 1)

104  Descartes, Rene Discourse on Method / Translator: John Veitch. Project Gutenberg online:  https://www.gutenberg.org/files/59/59-h/59-h.htm (Part III)

105  Descartes, Rene, *Meditations on First Philosophy* (1639) / Translated by John Cottingham (Second Meditation)  https://www.marxists.org/reference/archive/ descartes/1639/meditations.htm

106 Ibid.  https://www.marxists.org/reference/archive/descartes/1639/meditations. htm (First Meditation)

107 Descartes, Rene, *Discourse on Method* / Translator: John Veitch.  Project Gutenberg online::  https://www.gutenberg.org/files/59/59-h/59-h.htm (Part IV)

108 Descartes, Rene, *Meditations on First Philosophy* (1639) / Translated by John Cottingham  https://www.marxists.org/reference/archive/descartes/1639/ meditations.htm (Fourth Meditation)

### Kant

109 Kant, Immanuel *Answer the Question: What is Enlightenment?* / translated by D. Fidel Ferrer. Community Texts 2013.  https://archive.org/details/Answer-TheQuestionWhatIsEnlightenment/page/n1/mode/2up

110 Ibid.  https://archive.org/details/AnswerTheQuestionWhatIsEnlightenment/ page/n1/mode/2up

111 Ibid.  https://archive.org/details/AnswerTheQuestionWhatIsEnlightenment/ mode/2up

112 Kant, Immanuel *Grounding for the Metaphysics Of Morals* / translated by J. El-lington. Indianapolis/Cambridge: Hackett Publishing Co., Inc. 1981.  https:// archive.org/details/groundingformet000kant/page/n9/mode/2up

113 Ibid.  https://archive.org/details/groundworkofmeta0000kant/page/102/ mode/2up

114 Ibid.  https://archive.org/details/groundingformet000kant/page/30mode/2up

115 Kant, Immanuel Critique of Practical Reason / translated by Lewis White Beck. New Jersey:  Prentice Hall, Library or Liberal Arts 1993.  https://archive.org/ details/critiqueofpracti03edkant/page/168/mode/2up

### Kierkegaard

116 Hong, Howard & Edna, editors. The Essential Kierkegaard (p.207). New Jersey: Princeton University Press, 1995.  https://books.google.com/ books?id=WfvXAQAAQBAJ&pg=PA207

117 Kierkegaard, Soren *A Sickness Unto Death(p.57)* / edited by Howard and Edna Hong. New Jersey: Princeton University Press, 1980.  https://archive.org/ details/sicknessuntodeat00sren/page/56/mode/2up

118 Kierkegaard, Soren *Either/Or Part 2* (p.35) / edited by Howard and Edna Hong. New Jersey: Princeton University Press, 1980.:  https://archive.org/ details/eitherorpartiiki00sren/page/34/mode/2up

119 Ibid. (p.224). https://archive.org/details/eitherorpartiiki00sren/page/224/ mode/2up

120 Ibid. (p.86). https://archive.org/details/eitherorpartiiki00sren/page/86/ mode/2up

121 Holmes, Paul *On Kierkegaard and the Truth* (P.8) / edited by Gouwens, David & Barrett III, Lee. Oregon: Cascade Books, 2012. https://books.google.com/books?id=BHdJAwAAQBAJ&pg=PA8&lpg

122 Kierkegaard, Soren *Writings VI vol. 6: Fear and Trembling/Repetition* (p.34) / edited by Howard and Edna Hong. New Jersey: Princeton University Press, 1983. https://books.google.com/books?id=CqGaVuSXKbEC&pg=PA34&lpg

### Nietzsche

123 Nietzsche, Friedrich, *Ecce Homo* (page 40-41) / translated by R. J. Hollingdale. London: Penguin Books 1979. https://archive.org/details/eccehomohowonebe00niet_0/page/40/mode/2up

124 Nietzsche, Friedrich, *On The Genealogy of Morals* & *Ecce Homo* (p.272), Translated by Kauffman, Walter. New York: Vintage Books, 1967. https://archive.org/details/ongenealogyofmor00niet_0/page/272/mode/2up

125 Nietzsche, Friedrich, *Beyond Good and Evil* (p.68)/ translated by Walter Kauffman. New York: Vintage Books 1966. https://archive.org/details/beyondgoodevilpr00frie/page/68/mode/2up

126 Nietzsche, Friedrich, *Portable Nietzsche, Thus Spoke Zarathustra* / translated by Walter Kaufmann, (p. 269, Book 3, section 1, on the vision and the riddle). London: The Viking Press, 1957. https://archive.org/details/ThePortableNietzscheWalterKaufmann/page/n279/mode/2up

127 Nietzsche, Friedrich, *Twilight of the Idols* (p.479), Translated by Hollingdale, R.J. New York: Penguin Books, 1979. https://archive.org/details/twilightofidolsa00niet/page/74/mode/2up

128 Nietzsche, Friedrich, The *Genealogy of Morals* (p.13, ch. 1, sec. 7) / translated by Horace B. Samuel MA. New York: Boni & Liveright. https://archive.org/details/genealogyofmoral00nietuoft/page/12/mode/2up

129 Nietzsche, Friedrich, *Birth of Tragedy* (p. 3) / translated by Ronald Speirs, edited by Raymond Guess. UK: Cambridge University Press 1999. https://archive.org/details/birthoftragedyot00niet/page/n3

130 Nietzsche, Friedrich, *Portable Nietzsche (Zarathustra p. 152)*, translated by Walter Kaufmann. London: Penguin books, 1959. https://archive.org/details/ThePortableNietzscheWalterKaufmann/page/n163/mode/2up

131 Nietzsche, Friedrich, *Twilight of the Idols* (p.48) Translated by Hollingdale, R.J. Harmondsworth: Penguin Books, 1979. https://archive.org/details/twilightofidolsa00niet/page/n5/mode/2up

132 Nietzsche, Friedrich, *The Joyful Wisdom* / translated by Thomas Common, edited by Dr. Oscar Levy. New York: The Macmillan Co. 1924. "To 'give style' to one's character—a great and rare art! It is practiced by those who survey all the strengths and weaknesses of their nature and then fit them into an artistic plan until every one of them appears as art and reason and even weaknesses delight the eye." https://archive.org/details/completenietasch10nietuoft/page/222/mode/2up

133   Nietzsche, Friedrich, *Beyond Good and Evil* / translated by Walter Kauffman. New York: Vintage Books 1966.   https://archive.org/details/beyondgoodevil-pr00frie/page/n5

134   Nietzsche, Friedrich, *Twilight of the Idols* (p.74), Translated by Hollingdale, R.J. New York: Penguin Books, 1979.   https://archive.org/details/twilighto-fidolsa00niet/page/74/mode/2up

135   Nietzsche, Friedrich The Joyful Wisdom (p.270) / translated by Thomas Common, edited by Dr. Oscar Levy. New York: The Macmillan Co. 1924.   https://archive.org/details/completenietasch10nietuoft/page/270/mode/2up

136   Nietzsche, Friedrich, *Thus Spoke Zarathustra* (p.12) Translated by Common, Thomas. New York: Carlton House, 1967.   https://archive.org/details/in.er-net.dli.2015.209952/page/n21/mode/2up

137   Nietzsche, Friedrich, *The Birth of Tragedy* (p.6), Translated by Speirs, Ronald. UK: Cambridge University Press, 1999.   https://archive.org/details/birthof-tragedyot00niet/page/6/mode/2up

### *W. E. B. Du Bois*

138   Du Bois, W.E.B., *The Souls of Black Folk* (1903), "Of Our Spiritual Strivings"   https://www.gutenberg.org/files/408/408-h/408-h.htm

139   Ibid.   https://www.gutenberg.org/files/408/408-h/408-h.htm

140   Ibid.   https://www.gutenberg.org/files/408/408-h/408-h.htm

141   Ibid.   https://www.gutenberg.org/files/408/408-h/408-h.htm

142   Ibid.   https://www.gutenberg.org/files/408/408-h/408-h.htm

143   Ibid.   https://www.gutenberg.org/files/408/408-h/408-h.htm

144   Du Bois, W.E.B., *The Conservation of Races*, The American Negro Academy, Washington D.C." (1897)   https://www.gutenberg.org/files/31254/31254-h/31254-h.htm

145   Ibid.   https://www.gutenberg.org/files/31254/31254-h/31254-h.htm

146   Ibid.   Du Bois, W.E.B., *The Souls of Black Folk* (1903), "Of Our Spiritual Strivings"   https://www.gutenberg.org/files/408/408-h/408-h.htm

147   Ibid.   https://www.gutenberg.org/files/408/408-h/408-h.htm

148   Ibid.   Du Bois, W.E.B., *The Souls of Black Folk* (1903), "Of Mr. Booker T. and Others"   https://www.gutenberg.org/files/408/408-h/408-h.htm

149   Ibid.   Du Bois, W.E.B., *The Souls of Black Folk* (1903), "Of the Dawn of Freedom."   https://www.gutenberg.org/files/408/408-h/408-h.htm

150   Ibid.   Du Bois, W.E.B., *The Souls of Black Folk* (1903), "Of Our Spiritual Strivings"   https://www.gutenberg.org/files/408/408-h/408-h.htm

151   Ibid.   https://www.gutenberg.org/files/408/408-h/408-h.htm

...

152   Weil, Simone, *Simone Weil: Waiting For God [Letters and Essays]* (p.114) Translated by Crawford, Emma. New York: Capricorn Books, 1959, (p 456). https://archive.org/details/waitingforgodlet00weil/page/111/mode/2up

153   Ibid. (p.111). https://archive.org/details/waitingforgodlet00weil/page/111/mode/2up

154   Weil, Simone, *Selected Essays 1934-1943 Historical, Political and Moral Writings* (p.10,13), Translated by Richard Rees. Oregon: Wipf & Stock, 2015.

155   Ibid. (p.27)

156   Weil, Simone, *Gravity and Grace* (p.111) Translated by Crawford, Emma and von der Ruhr, M. London: Routledge and Keegan Paul, 1952.   https://archive.org/details/gravitygrace0000weil/page/111/mode/2up

157   Ibid.   https://archive.org/details/gravitygrace0000weil/page/111/mode/2up

158   Weil, Simone, *Waiting For God [Letters and Essays]* (p.114) Translated by Crawford, Emma. New York: Capricorn Books, 1959.   https://archive.org/details/waitingforgodlet00weil/page/114/mode/2up

159   Weil, Simone, *Simone Weil, an Anthology* (p.65) Edited by Sian Miles. New York: Weidenfeld and Nicholson, 1986.   https://archive.org/details/simoneweilanthol0000weil/page/65/mode/2up

160   Caranfa, Angelo, *Beauty and Grace* (Claudel on *Weil and Grace* p.73). Toronto & London: Associated University Press, 1989.

161   Weil, Simone, *Gravity and Grace* (p.1) Translated by Crawford, Emma and von der Ruhr, M. London: Routledge and Keegan Paul, 1952.   https://archive.org/details/gravitygrace0000weil/page/n39/mode/2up

162   Weil, Simone, *Simone Weil, an Anthology* (p.270) Edited by Sian Miles. New York: Weidenfeld and Nicholson, 1986.   https://archive.org/details/simoneweilanthol0000weil/page/270/mode/2up

163   Weil, Simone, *The Notebooks of Simone Weil* (p.290) Translated by Arthur Wills. London & New York: Routledge, Taylor and Francis Group, 1956.

164   Weil, Simone, *Simone Weil, an Anthology* (p.273) Edited by Sian Miles. New York: Weidenfeld and Nicholson, 1986.   https://archive.org/details/simoneweilanthol0000weil/page/273/mode/2up

165   Weil, Simone, *Waiting For God [Letters and Essays]* (p.151) Translated by Crawford, Emma. New York: Capricorn Books, 1959.   https://archive.org/details/waitingforgodlet00weil/page/151/mode/2up

166   Weil, Simone, *Gravity and Grace* (p.145) Translated by Crawford, Emma and von der Ruhr, M. London: Routledge and Keegan Paul, 1952.   https://archive.org/details/gravitygrace0000weil/page/145/mode/2up

167   Weil, Simone, *Gravity and Grace* (p.135) Translated by Crawford, Emma and von der Ruhr, M. London: Routledge and Keegan Paul, 1952.   https://archive.org/details/gravitygrace0000weil/page/135/mode/2up

168 Arendt, Hannah, *Eichmann In Jerusalem* (p.252). NY: Viking Press, 1964. https://archive.org/details/eichmanninjerusa00aren/page/252/mode/2up

169 Arendt, Hannah, *Thinking without a Banister: Essays in Understanding*, 1953-1975, Schocken, 2018, pg. 473.

170 Arendt, Hannah: Responsibility and Judgement (Edited by Kohn). 2003, Schopenhauer Books, New York.pg.45. https://archive.org/details/responsibilityju0000aren/mode/2up/search/that+silent+dialogue+between+me+and+myself+

171 Arendt, Hannah, Eichmann In Jerusalem (p.252). NY: Viking Press, 1964. https://archive.org/details/eichmanninjerusa00aren/page/252/mode/2up

172 Ibid. (p.126). https://archive.org/details/eichmanninjerusa00aren/page/126/mode/2up

173 Ibid. (p.114). https://archive.org/details/eichmanninjerusa00aren/page/114/mode/2up

174 Ibid. (p. 64) https://archive.org/details/cambridgecompani00vill/page/64/mode/2up/search/Eichmann+in+Jerusalem

175 Arendt, Hannah, *The Life of the Mind*. New York: Harcourt, Brace & Jovanovich, Inc., 1977. FREE ONLINE AT https://archive.org/details/lifeofmind01aren/page/4/mode/2up/search/it+was+not+stupidity+but+thoughtlessness

176 Arendt, Hannah. *The Jewish Writings* (edited by Kohn & Feldman), The Literary Trust; 2007 Schoken Books, New York.

177 Arendt, Hannah & Mary McCarthy *Between friends : the correspondence of Hannah Arendt and Mary McCarthy, 1949-1975* (p.149). NY: Harcourt Brace, 1995. https://archive.org/details/betweenfriendsco00aren/page/149/mode/2up?q=the+proportions+of+a+pogrom

### Jean-Paul Sartre

178 Kaufman, Walter [ed. / translator] *Existentialism from Dostoevsky to Sartre* [section: Sartre, Jean Paul: Existentialism is a Humanism]. New York: Penguin/Meridian Books, 1975. https://archive.org/details/isbn_9780452009301/page/352/mode/2up

179 Ibid. https://archive.org/details/isbn_9780452009301/page/344/mode/2up

180 Ibid. https://archive.org/details/isbn_9780452009301/page/344/mode/2up

181 Ibid. https://archive.org/details/isbn_9780452009301/page/349/mode/2up

182 Ibid. https://archive.org/details/isbn_9780452009301/page/344/mode/2up

183 Ibid. https://archive.org/details/isbn_9780452009301/page/368/mode/2up

184 Ibid. https://archive.org/details/isbn_9780452009301/page/344/mode/2up

185  Ibid.  https://archive.org/details/isbn_9780452009301/page/358/mode/2up

186  Ibid.  https://archive.org/details/isbn_9780452009301/page/344/mode/2up

187  Emerson, Ralph Waldo, *Self Reliance* (p.13). New York: Peter Pauper Press, 1967.  https://archive.org/details/selfreliance00emer/page/13/mode/2up

### Simone De Beauvoir

188  De Beauvoir, Simone *Ethics of Ambiguity* (p. 91). Translated by Frechtman, Bernard. NY: Citadel Press, 1976   https://archive.org/details/ethicsofambiguit00beau/page/90/mode/2up

189  Ibid. (p.127).   https://archive.org/details/ethicsofambiguit00beau/page/127/mode/2up

190  Ibid. (p.28).   https://archive.org/details/ethicsofambiguit00beau/page/28/mode/2up

191  De Beauvoir, Simone *The Second Sex* (p.17) / translated by C. Borde & S. Malovaney. New York: Vintage eBooks, 2010.   https://archive.org/details/1949SimoneDeBeauvoirTheSecondSex/page/n17/mode/2up

192  Ibid. (p.12).   https://archive.org/details/ethicsofambiguit00beau/page/12/mode/2up

193  De Beauvoir, Simone *Ethics of Ambiguity* (p.51). New York: Citadel Press, 1976.   https://archive.org/details/ethicsofambiguit00beau/page/51/mode/2up

194  Ibid. (p.66)   https://archive.org/details/ethicsofambiguit00beau/page/66/mode/2up?q=fulfilled

195  Ibid. (p.72).   https://archive.org/details/ethicsofambiguit00beau/page/72/mode/2up

196  Ibid. (p.86).   https://archive.org/details/ethicsofambiguit00beau/page/86/mode/2up

197  Ibid. (p.82).   https://archive.org/details/ethicsofambiguit00beau/page/82/mode/2up

198  Ibid. (p.66).   https://archive.org/details/ethicsofambiguit00beau/page/66/mode/2up

199  Ibid. (p.134). "In setting up its ends, freedom must put them in parentheses, confront them at each moment with that absolute end which it itself constitutes, and contest, in its own name, the means it uses to win itself."   https://archive.org/details/ethicsofambiguit00beau/page/134/mode/2up

200  Ibid. (p.67).   https://archive.org/details/ethicsofambiguit00beau/page/67/mode/2up

### Albert Camus

201  Camus, Albert *The Myth of Sisyphus and Other Essays* / translated by Justin O'Brien. New York: Vintage Books 1955.   https://archive.org/details/mythofsisyphusot0000camu_j4j5/page/14/mode/2up

202 Ibid. https://archive.org/dctails/mythofsisyphusot0000camu_j4j5/page/60/mode/2up

203 Ibid. https://archive.org/details/mythofsisyphusot0000camu_j4j5/page/14/mode/2up

204 Ibid. https://archive.org/details/mythofsisyphusot0000camu_j4j5/page/6/mode/2up

205 Ibid. https://archive.org/details/mythofsisyphusot0000camu_j4j5/page/14/mode/2up

206 Ibid. https://archive.org/details/mythofsisyphusot0000camu_j4j5/page/1/mode/2up

207 Ibid. https://archive.org/details/mythofsisyphusot0000camu_j4j5/page/55/mode/2up

208 Ibid. https://archive.org/details/mythofsisyphusot0000camu_j4j5/page/62/mode/2up

209 Ibid. https://archive.org/details/mythofsisyphusot0000camu_j4j5/page/58/mode/2up

210 Ibid. https://archive.org/details/mythofsisyphusot0000camu_j4j5/page/94/mode/2up

211 Ibid. https://archive.org/details/mythofsisyphusot0000camu_j4j5/page/120/mode/2up

212 Ibid. https://archive.org/details/mythofsisyphusot0000camu_j4j5/page/121/mode/2up

213 Ibid. https://archive.org/details/mythofsisyphusot0000camu_j4j5/page/121/mode/2up

214 Ibid. https://archive.org/details/mythofsisyphusot0000camu_j4j5/page/57/mode/2up

215 Sartre, Jean-Paul *Tribute to Camus* from *The Reporter Magazine,* February 4, 1960, p. 34. Copyright 1960 by *The Reporter Magazine* Company. Translated by Justin O'Brien.

216 Camus, Albert *The Myth of Sisyphus and Other Essays* / translated by Justin O'Brien. New York: Vintage Books 1955. https://archive.org/details/mythofsisyphusot0000camu_j4j5/page/60/mode/2up

### Frantz Fanon

217 Lewis, Gordon. Denean, Sharpley-Whiting & White Editors. *Fanon: A Critical Reader* (p.116). Oxford, UK, Blackwell Publishers Ltd., 1996 . https://archive.org/details/fanoncriticalrea0000unse/page/116/mode/2up

218 Fanon, Frantz, *Black Skin, White Masks* (p.112). New York: Grove Press, Inc., 1967. https://archive.org/details/blackskinwhitema00fano/page/112/mode/2up

219 Fanon, Frantz *The Wretched of the Earth* (p.36) / Translated by Richard Philcox. New York: Grove Press, 1965. https://archive.org/details/revhosatx46/page/n36/mode/2up

220 Fanon, Frantz, *Black Skin, White Masks* (p.114). New York: Grove Press, Inc, 1967. https://archive.org/details/blackskinwhitema00fano/page/114/mode/2up

221 Ibid. (p.116). https://archive.org/details/blackskinwhitema00fano/page/116/mode/2up

222 Ibid. (p.232). https://archive.org/details/blackskinwhitema00fano/page/232/mode/2up

223 Ibid. (p.123). https://archive.org/details/blackskinwhitema00fano/page/123/mode/2up

224 Ibid. (p.114). https://archive.org/details/blackskinwhitema00fano/page/114/mode/2up

225 Fanon, Frantz, *The Wretched of the Earth* (p.53) / Translated by Richard Philcox. New York: Grove Press, 1965. https://archive.org/details/revhosatx46/page/n36/mode/2up

226 Ibid. https://archive.org/details/revhosatx46/page/n36/mode/2up

227 Ibid. (p.1) https://archive.org/details/revhosatx46/page/n36/mode/2up

228 Ibid. (p.2) https://archive.org/details/revhosatx46/page/n36/mode/2up

229 Ibid. (p.44) https://archive.org/details/revhosatx46/page/n36/mode/2up

### Gloria Anzaldua

230 Ashcroft, Bill, Griffiths, G, Tiffin, H. Editors, *The Post Colonial Studies Reader,* 2nd Edition (p.208). London and New York: Routledge, 1995.

231 Hernandez, Leandra and Gutierrez, Robert, *The Bridge We Call Communication: Anzalduan Approaches to Theory, Method and Praxis* (p.148). Lanham, MD: Lexington Books, 2019.

232 Anzaldua, Gloria, *(La Prieta) The Gloria Anzaldua Reader* (p.45), Edited by Ana Louise Keating. Durham: Duke University Press, 2009.

233 Ifekwunigwe, Jayne, *'Mixed Race' Studies: A Reader* (p.140). London and New York: Routledge, 2004

234 Anzaldua, Gloria, *The Gloria Anzaldua Reader* (p.2), Edited by Ana Louise Keating. Durham: Duke University Press, 2009.

235 Bhavnani, Kum-Kum, *Feminism and 'Race'* (p.98). Oxford/New York: Oxford University Press, 2001.

236 Anzaldua, Gloria, *Borderlands/La Frontera.* New York: Aunt Lute Books, 1987.

237 Herndl-Prince, Diane, *Feminism Redux: An Anthology of Literary Theory and Criticism* (p.309). New York: Rutgers University Press, 2009.

238  Wendland, Joel, *The Collectivity of Life: Spaces of Social Mobility and the Individualism Myth* (p.76). Lanham, MD: Lexington Books, 2016.

239  Martin, Holly, *Writing Between Cultures: A Study of Hybrid Narratives In Ethnic Literature of the United States* (p.89). North Carolina: McFarland & Co., 2011.

240  Anzaldua, Gloria, *The Gloria Anzaldua Reader* (p.73), Edited by Ana Louise Keating. Durham: Duke University Press, 2009.

241  Anzaldua, Gloria, *Borderlands/La Frontera*. New York: Aunt Lute Books, 1987.

## SHARIN N. ELKHOLY, PhD

### FACULTY PAGE UNIVERSITY OF HOUSTON—DOWNTOWN

https://www.uhd.edu/academics/humanities/undergraduate-programs/philosophy/Pages/bio-ElkholyS.aspx


### SHARIN N. ELKHOLY PHILOSOPHY WISE WEBSITE

philosophywise.com

This book was composed using the typefaces
Heldane Text and Heldane Display, designed
by Kris Sowersby in 2018 and distributed
by Klim Type Foundry.

Made in the USA
Coppell, TX
16 January 2023

11148294R00125